CUSTOMER OBSESSION

How to Acquire, Retain, and Grow
Customers in the New Age of
Relationship Marketing

ABAETÊ DE AZEVEDO
AND
RICARDO POMERANZ

New York   Chicago   San Francisco   Lisbon   London
Madrid   Mexico City   Milan   New Delhi   San Juan
Seoul   Singapore   Sydney   Toronto

1 2 3 4 5 6 7 8 9 0   FGR/FGR   0 1 0 9 8

ISBN: 978–0–07–149704–6
MHID: 0–07–149704–8

Printed and bound by QuebecorWorld.

McGraw-Hill books are available at special quantity discounts to use as premiums and sales promotions, or for use in corporate training programs. To contact a representative please visit the Contact Us pages at www.mhprofessional.com.

We dedicate this book

To my patient, good-humored, and affectionate wife, Juçara U. de Azevedo, and my infallible English dictionary. To my children, Jacyara, Iberê, and Acauã, from whom I get the oxygen for my best energy. To Atám, brother, father, and best friend. And also Dorinha's enthusiastic kindness.

ABAETÊ

To my wife, Cristiane, who has taught me the real meaning of the word relationship, not only in the corporate world, but in life. To my children, Yuri, Bruno, and Larissa, who are the main reasons for my achievements. To Noelli, Loris, Lenina, and Carl, who are always cheering me on.

RICARDO

Acknowledgements

This book has had important personal contributions, both local and international.

André Pasquali was in charge of art direction, providing us with his creative talent and great work capacity to create and diagram the content. Maurício Castro da Silva reviewed the financial math required to make some of the more involved technical calculations.

Marcos Yamamura coordinated the gathering of on-line illustrations and Mauro Letízia was responsible for selecting the most representative options. Juliana Verde, Leila Braz, Marcos Bittencourt, Marianna Capobianco and Tatiana Pacheco helped in obtaining approval from the clients.

Ágatha Bellesso's support was also decisive in managing the various daily support activities that require so much time and organization. We also want to acknowledge Acauã Azevedo for an excellent suggestion.

Several marketing professionals also contributed and are responsible for choosing the brand cases. Here we want to thank the executives Antônio Matias, Emílio Munaro, Fábio Bruggioni, Fernando Chacon, Flávio Dias, Flávio Lima, Guilherme Franco, Jacuguara Santos, Jaime Chaves, Marcos Nohur, Mirian Huchigara, Paulo Gouvêa, Sérgio Santos, Simone Dinis and Vinicius Carraro.

Direct from Omnicom NY, Carmem Baez led the requests for cases from the 70 Rapp Collins Worldwide agencies, with Tais Melilo's operational support. And from our Rapp Collins Latino-Americana, we had the collaboration of Maximo Rainuzzo from Argentina and Paul Garnier from Costa Rica.

And for encouragement and guidance, we want to thank Milton Assumpção and also Ernesto Yoshida for his support.

Contents

Introduction

Reality shows us that both the strategy and practice of marketing communication are much more complex than what has been depicted in the marketing literature. This book seeks to develop some new thinking about the issue. The perspective is innovative, based on the observation of hundreds of success stories, some of which are discussed in the following chapters. This book argues for the integration of communication disciplines from a relationship-marketing point of view, which involves segmenting the target users according to their value for the brand and treating communication as an *ongoing, interconnected process* rather than a series of isolated events. The different stages of the relationship with each individual—awareness, consideration, conversion, and postsale—shape the message and determine the most appropriate marketing channels. Directed communication gains a positive reputation for quality and value and provides support for brand building, which, in turn, helps generate sales.

Relationship marketing's focus is on maximizing the return on investments in the brand. This book intends to demonstrate the validity of the following equation: relationship marketing = results marketing. One is the means, and the other is the end. They are different sides to the same problem: the search for maximum returns on marketing investments.

Reference

This book is organized as a sequence of topics that permit the reader to easily understand the fundamental practices and concepts of relationship marketing. To explore the practical aspects of adopting this approach, processes, methodologies, tools, and case studies are based on those of one of the most representative global relationship-marketing agency networks, Rapp Collins. It is thus possible to match the theoretical aspects of results marketing with its implementation in the company's everyday activities.

Structure

Chapter 1 introduces the evolving perspective of communication strategies over the past 100 years. It emphasizes that the current moment has imposed limitations on conventional marketing practices and that in order to respond effectively to the new competitive environment, it is necessary to reassess the concepts of public, channel, and communication. Chapter 2 discusses the issue of customer value, making it very clear that every customer occupies a different position, and that some offer more profits than others. After that, Chapter 3 details the main types of marketing programs based on the different stages of customers' relationship with the brands. Chapter 4 focuses on choosing the appropriate channel, underscoring the importance of integrating marketing communication starting with the relationship-marketing strategy. Chapter 5 concludes the theoretical presentation by elaborating on the correct communication method for obtaining results.

The next four chapters concentrate on the practical aspects of implementing a new communication model. Chapter 6 analyzes the processes and infrastructure necessary for implementing relationship-marketing programs. Chapter 7 addresses the use of databases as a support tool for storing the public's individualized information and for creating predictive models. Chapter 8 describes the ROI calculation models for measuring financial returns on marketing investments. Chapter 9 presents summaries of cases involving several worldwide brands, all of which illustrate themes discussed in the preceding chapters. The book concludes with Chapter 10, which demonstrates that relationship marketing is a global trend today with a strong perspective for growth over the next few years. The objective of the appendix, entitled "Insights on Customers through Segmentation," is to enrich the discussion of database intelligence and construction, which is introduced in Chapter 7. It looks at a project developed for an American telecommunications company with the goal of demonstrating how segmentation of the target public helps marketing.

Who Is This Book For?

This book was written with the goal of becoming a useful tool for business professionals and executives, marketing managers, communications professionals, and business students in undergraduate, graduate, and MBA programs—in other words, anyone who is interested in understanding the changing nature of brands from a new perspective, one informed by the analysis of new results provided by relationship marketing.

CHAPTER 1

Industry, Retail, or the Consumer: Who Controls the Market?

There is a historical relationship among industry, retail, and the consumer. The objective of this chapter is to show that the main theme of this book—how to maximize results through relationship-marketing strategies—is the most recent stage of the evolution of communication among these three entities and the market.

Over the past 100 years, the relationship among the members of this triad has undergone profound change, with competition as the backdrop. Industry was the first to rule, followed by retail, and finally the consumer. In this new scenario, relationship marketing has begun to play a fundamental role in how these entities interact. Over the next few pages, we'll share the changes over time in the roles of these three pillars of the value distribution system for the market and provide an analysis of the accompanying role of marketing's communication mix throughout this evolution.

Low Supply, High Demand: Industry Focused on Products

At the beginning of the twentieth century in the United States, when big industry began to emerge, the pioneer products in their categories needed only to announce their arrival at the stores.

Retail and consumers were anxiously awaiting the novelties that would bring comfort and practicality. Demand was latent, and choices were nonexistent. Industry was in control of the market. Without any competitors within a particular category, industry produced new products according to the laws of economies of scale. A classic example of this industrial supremacy occurred in 1908 when Ford launched the Model T, the first automobile in the world to be produced in series. In order to reduce costs, the cars left the assembly line painted exclusively black. Legend has it that Henry Ford told the American consumers that they could buy the Model T in any color they wanted—so long as it was black.

During the first half of the twentieth century, the first department stores emerged, driven by technological advances in transportation that made it possible for consumers to travel longer distances to acquire products. The relationship between retail and consumers had undergone its first quantitative change. The range and service capacity of the local stores did not include more than a few dozen buyers, but department stores now reached in the hundreds. However, the marketing strategy still consisted of establishing long-term personal relationships with consumers, thus ensuring their return to the stores.

The Model T was a success. However, after selling nearly 15 million units in the following decades, Ford's sales suddenly fell sharply. One of the reasons was that other car manufacturers, like General Motors, had begun to offer cars with other color options. This phenomenon did not occur exclusively in the automobile segment. After the first half of the twentieth century, and until the 1980s, the new marketing strategy for industry was to focus on the efficiency of distribution channels with the objective of serving the highest number of consumers possible. The market was avid to consume, and industry responded in proportion to expectations. This was the great growth period for the product industries. According to Vavra,[1] "only one type of Tide detergent was sold from 1947 to 1984. In 1985, Procter & Gamble introduced four new types. Crest toothpaste was available in more than 100 different combinations of package, flavor and size, and Campbell's introduced four new brands of canned soups in the end of the 1980s."

The Search for Increased Supply: Retail Gains Space

As part of this new logic, industry began to direct its production to some distributors, which in turn used large numbers of resellers to reach the end users. In general, these resellers consisted of small points of sale spread around a large geographical area, which allowed greater access to the consumer base. This is when shopping malls began to emerge and retail stores began to reach tens of thousands of consumers.

At that time, marketing strategy was characterized by the use of media and mass merchandising. In the 1960s, the emphasis was on a product's appeal to a homogeneous base of consumers. Over the next two decades, companies identified the market potential of niches and began to develop products for more specific segments. Near the end of the 1970s, customer service support systems using the telephone (the so-called 1-800 toll-free number) emerged. These systems, together with the credit cards created in the 1950s, gave catalog and telemarketing sales a tremendous boost. These new channels had the capacity to reach hundreds of thousands of people. In the beginning of the 1990s, with the arrival of the superstores, this consumer base now extended beyond a few million users.

Much has changed since the times of the neighborhood five-and-dime store, where the owner knew the preference of every one of his few dozen customers and used to attend to them by name. Visiting points of sale by the thousands every day, consumers have changed their profiles and their relationships with retail. Store owners began to buy millions of dollars worth of goods from the industries and sell millions of dollars worth of goods to consumers. A great diversity of products supplied by several manufacturers with countless shape, color, and resource options began to appear within the same category. This made it possible for the stores to begin to negotiate with industries, buying and reselling only the most profitable products in each category.

In this new phase, characterized by the increased number of competitors offering similar products, the power axis began to shift from industry to retail. Retail gained tremendous bargaining power because, on the one hand, it was able to buy from a vast range of different suppliers, and, on the other, it had direct access to an immense number of consumers. Retailers could negotiate with the industry they were interested in working with.

The logic that allowed the efficient expansion of markets through the creation of a sophisticated distribution system is ironically the same as the logic that put industry in a delicate growth situation. Retail started to change from a mere product sales channel into a relationship centralizer with the consumer. As a result, retail does not link up exclusively with any one brand. Instead, the products that receive the greatest consumer acceptance and provide the best returns will be positioned in the most advantageous places in the stores. An extreme example of this dynamic occurred when large retail companies created their own brands, thus becoming their own suppliers' direct competitors.

More Demanding Consumers and Direct Relationship Channels

A few decades of accelerated industrialization have passed, causing a tremendous sociocultural impact on an ever more consumption-minded society that nevertheless is more demanding in its choices.

Consumers are more mature and more aware of the available options. In addition to product quality, they demand solutions that are more convenient. The end of the twentieth century saw the arrival of sales channels that changed the logistics of commerce, such as home shopping. Whether by telemarketing or the Internet, consumers—seated in the privacy of their own homes—can now search for products, compare benefits and prices, place their orders, and have the merchandise delivered directly to their doorstep. They can also choose the precise payment method, revolutionizing the financial system, which actually had to restructure itself to provide support to the new consumer profile. Home shopping caused a veritable revolution in industry's relations with retail and retail's relations with the consumer.

This opening of new sales channels with the consumer, which basically added to the store's physical space, provided a chance for industry to recover lost ground in its relationship with its consumer base. Although most manufacturers continue to use resellers as their entire distribution structure, new direct sales models have emerged. One of the most representative cases is Dell, the world leader in direct sales of computer systems.[2] Dell's business model was pioneering: completely bypassing the retail intermediary, it offered a personalized relationship with corporate and institutional customers, but it also enabled general consumers to purchase directly over the Internet (currently with an average volume of $50 million in daily sales) and to have customized orders to meet individual demands. Technical assistance, along with other services, is provided over the phone or online.

The beginning of the new millennium signaled a new phase in marketing, with market control going into the hands of the consumer. And the marketing industry consistently responded by making this relationship with the consumer a priority. Direct marketing,[3] or relationship marketing, as it came to be known, grew dramatically in importance. *Relationship marketing* can be defined as the communication discipline that plans and creates individualized and personalized communication actions with the objective of obtaining a direct reply from the consumer and maintaining a long-term relationship with him or her.

Recovering the Consumer Market through Relationship Marketing

Relationship marketing seeks a direct dialogue with a brand's customers. *Relationship* suggests an action-reaction dynamic. In order to communicate an appropriate and effective message, one that will speak to each customer and compel a response, one must know the target public, its consumption preferences, its personal habits, and its sociocultural values. Without knowing all these details about the consumer, there is no way to personalize communication. You run the risk of not attracting consumers' attention, thereby drastically reducing the number of responses.

Mass-marketing campaigns have traditionally been industry's first spontaneous investment. With this strategy, the focus is on increasing sales volume by reaching the largest audience possible. In mature markets, however, investments in relationship marketing have been around for a longer period of time; that is why these marketers already have accumulated experience. For example, it is known that among the consumers of a specific brand, only about 20 percent are responsible for the purchase of 80 percent of total volume. This is an internationally accepted principle called the Pareto law.

If that's the case, then the quality of the consumer is more important than the quantity, and it is vital to know just who these more valuable consumers are. That's why many companies invest in mapping their consumer base. By identifying and classifying their customers based on their individual value for the brand, they can make investments proportional to the importance of each customer and carry out specific relationship campaigns. They can then monitor and administer these investments and once again gain greater control of their market—not through the product this time, but through the consumer.

The beginning of the twenty-first century presented an extremely competitive scenario for companies. The products launched on the market are still very similar. And while many organizations' research departments play a fundamental role in developing innovative solutions, these solutions remain original for only a short period, until a similar proposal reaches the market. With regard to retail, there is an exaggerated availability of shopping malls and stores. According to Rapp and Collins,[4] in the 1990s there were already nearly 35,000 shopping malls in the United States, many of which were operating partially empty. Price wars are not a long-term alternative, since competitors immediately lower the prices of similar products, thus canceling out the effects of the initial attempt. This downward spiral may lead to situations of financial unsustainability for many companies, implying a return to original prices or even the removal of the solution from the market.

In addition, the search for new distribution places is becoming increasingly difficult in a globalized economy in which local companies are not the only competition and more businesses find themselves also dealing with better-prepared global rivals. In many cases, the alternative for a competitive differential ends up being based on the promotional component of the marketing mix. In response, companies try to maintain a presence and a preference in the minds of consumers by spending ever larger amounts of capital. They direct their communication to the largest number of people possible. However, the mass-marketing strategy encounters totally adverse conditions compared to those in the last half of the twentieth century, when this strategy had a direct impact on sales of new products. The consumer, bombarded by all kinds of media messages, does not respond as expected. A study from Ball State University underscores that Americans are exposed to an average of nine hours of media every day. Many companies attempt to solve the low consumer response issue by increasing their investments in new communications to even higher levels, further feeding the reasons behind the poor results.

In response to such intense competition, marketers are creating strategies that closely parallel the new power relationships between industry, retail, and consumers. We are now in the midst of a new era in which the companies that count on consumer relationship programs will once again gain control. However, this differs from the small store marketing strategy at the beginning of the twentieth century; the new challenge that companies face is establishing individualized relationships with a consumer base that has grown exponentially. This is called mass customized marketing.

In this new environment, it is necessary to establish very precise strategies regarding the consumer base you wish to reach; the products and services you are offering to this base; the channels used; and the application of managerial, technological, and more efficient distribution processes to guarantee the best return on invested capital. Companies that understand and know how to apply the new relationship-marketing strategies will recover the control they lost through the complexity of the existing competitive setting.

This new era demands that both industry and retail shift the axis of their marketing actions, which in the past have focused on the products and services being offered, to those issues related to the consumer, who is beginning to control the relationship with the company. The consumer has become the beginning and the end for each product and brand, defining the most convenient channels for interaction, the periodicity with which he or she wants to receive new contacts, and the expected speed of response in relation to these very issues. There are cases in which consumers even define the product, such as on Nike's site (www.nikeid.com), where users create their own shoe, specially defined according to their profile, by choosing from an enormous combination of models and colors.

Once the desired consumer base has been mapped, relationship marketing uses communication mechanisms to attract the user's response and begin a dialogue. In this stage, the user has the option to select the most appropriate direct channel to develop this relationship. This can be by phone, point of sale, multimedia kiosks, the Internet, PDAs, interactive TV, game consoles, among others. The key is providing the most convenient channel for the consumer. Companies can then record information for this process in a database called the Consumer Information Center (CIC). Some examples of relevant attributes are: name, address, telephone number, products of interest, purchase date, and amount spent.

This information will provide, first, a more precise identification of user categories based on the users' purchase propensity standards, and second, the elaboration of new personalized communication actions. In this latter case, as the consumer interacts with the brand, his or her preferences are recorded, which in turn allows companies to create a customized and individualized communication. The new information is added to the CIC. This learning relationship, already identified by Peppers and Rogers,[5] establishes and consolidates the basis for customer loyalty thanks to the convenience of the process and the difficulty and high costs involved should the individual wish to switch to a competitor's brand. Each of these communication actions must be measured in relation to their marketing results based on previously planned metrics. This permits the continuous fine-tuning of the actions and the maximization of returns on investment throughout the consumer's life cycle (see Figure 1.1).

Figure 1.1 The Relationship-Marketing Process

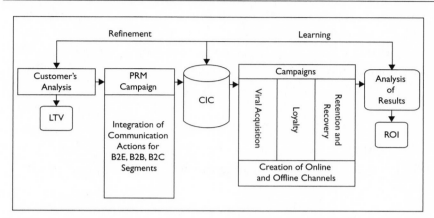

The objective of the following chapters is to introduce each of the steps in relationship marketing in more detail and to show the vast range of companies in several categories—such as corporate communities, service retailers, and consumer goods retailers and industries—that have successfully used this strategy of dialogue with the consumer.

Key Points

- Over the past 100 years, the power relationship among industry, retail, and the consumer, the three pillars of the value distribution system for the market, has undergone profound change. Control was first in the hands of industry, then of retail, and finally, of the consumer. At the beginning of the twentieth century, pioneer industries had control of the market for their categories. The product offerings were low, and there was no pressure from competition.
- From the middle of the century to the 1980s, industry began to benefit from the efficiency of the distribution

channels with the objective of expanding its consumer universe. A large diversity of products supplied by several manufacturers emerged within the same category.

- With the increase in the number of competitors, the power axis began to shift from industry to retail. Retail obtained tremendous bargaining power and was no longer a mere product sales channel, but had become a relationship centralizer with the consumer. The latter matured and became increasingly more demanding.
- Thanks to the emergence of new sales channels, such as home shopping, the consumer can now buy products and receive merchandise without leaving home. This led to growth in the importance of relationship marketing, which plans and creates individualized and personalized communication actions to maintain long-term relationships with the consumer, maximizing the return for the brand.
- To recover the control lost because of increased competition, companies need to shift the axis of their marketing actions, which in the past were centralized on a product and advertising perspective, to a focus on dialogue and communication with the consumer, who has become the beginning and the end of results marketing for each product and brand.

CHAPTER 2

How Much Is Each Customer Worth?

It is common practice in marketing to group customers together based on their needs. By understanding the reasons why each group buys a company's products or services, it is possible to create a more direct and objective communication approach for each segment. However, segmentation based exclusively on what customers want is not sufficient to enable a company to maximize its return on its investments in marketing.

Each Customer Has a Value for the Brand

Individuals with exactly the same needs can provide completely different financial results for a brand. For example, there are those who buy more regularly and become a greater source of income. The same thing happens in relation to purchase indications. Some individuals recommend products or services that they like to others in their circle. They not only acquire the merchandise, but they will also spread the word about its advantages, thus increasing the chances for new sales. On the other hand, there are consumers who need constant support from customer service centers for the installation, use, or maintenance of the product, thus having a negative impact on the cost curve.

When comparing the latter with the group that requires minimal support, it is very evident which segment is financially more advantageous to the company. Booz Allen & Hamilton conducted a study that showed that while the cost per banking transaction was around $1.07 for service at brick-and-mortar sites, the same service offered by the telephone call center fell to $0.54, and if it was offered over the Internet, it fell to $0.01.[1]

Individuals, regardless of their particular consumer needs, have different values for companies. Plainly and simply, some customers just offer more profit than others! Whether this is due to their impact on income or on expenses, the maximization of returns on marketing actions will be achieved only when the company takes this dimension into account when developing its communication strategy. It is important to distinguish the most valuable customers and to create differentiated offers and services for them. Treating the base in a homogeneous manner in relation to value means disregarding the different cash flows that result from each profile.

The main strategies that companies use to obtain the highest return possible from marketing investments correspond to the following three types:

1. *Value maximization based on the product or service.* Some companies seek to maximize their financial return by concentrating their marketing efforts on selling their products. Their starting point is their merchandise portfolio. Since profitability is based on the profit margin that results from sales, these companies focus on maximizing sales volume. They disregard the individual value of each customer in the process, not understanding the full extension of the profitability function.
2. *Value maximization based on share of pocket.* Other companies base their actions on the customer's spending potential (share of pocket). Knowing each individual's spending potential as well as the value of his or her recent purchases, they concentrate their

marketing actions on the more important segments—specifically, the groups with the highest purchase potential and the least amount of recently acquired products. There are bigger opportunities here, so time and monetary investment resources should preferably be directed to this area.

Computer manufacturer marketers have used the share of pocket concept in marketing to the corporate market. They map the average number of computers per employee in each target sector. Large, medium, and small companies are assigned different values based on their earnings level. With the help of research tools, it is possible to find out the actual number of machines that each company owns and identify where there is potential for growth. The difference between the actual number of computers owned by each company and the average number owned by companies with similar earnings in the same sector creates an ordered list of companies that have the greatest spending potential.

3. *Value maximization based on lifetime value.* Customer value throughout the entire period that a specific individual generates income before abandoning the brand should be estimated. This has to be done from the first to the last purchase. Companies calculate that number by considering all future profit flows, based on the transactions and deducting the respective costs. After finding the present values and adding them, the final number represents the customer's monetary value, also called lifetime value, or LTV.

There are different ways to calculate LTV, ranging from rudimentary models to sophisticated modeling techniques. In general, for each customer you should add all sales made and subtract the costs of the products and directly related services, administrative overhead, promotional communication costs, and any discounts. In some cases, this information is not available because of the distribution structure that has been created, with retail retaining all knowledge of consumer purchases. In other cases, the information is difficult to measure, as in the case of overhead costs that have been aggregated, rather than broken down by individual purchase.

When it is impossible to make the calculation for each customer, the solution generally adopted is to use average LTV values, obtained by dividing the company's profitability by the total number of buyers throughout their life cycle. As we will see later in this chapter, the final result in this case is incomplete for segmentation purchases, but it is still a valuable indicator, helping companies to determine the financial status of their businesses.

There are enormous advantages to implementing individualized calculations. First, it allows a company to figure out when it makes sense to allocate more resources to obtain new consumers. If communication costs are higher than the LTV for new buyers, the action is not justified, since the company will incur negative returns on investment. This goes against the idea that the more customers a company has, the better its business is. It is not enough to simply attract lots of customers. They must also spend enough to allow the company to turn a profit.

Identifying, in time, high-LTV consumers with a propensity to abandon the brand can help the company to avoid losing out on significant earnings. In recovery programs, the same resources are often allocated to the entire base of discontented customers in a homogeneous way. But those with lower LTVs should have less priority. Those with negative LTVs should be disregarded altogether in making marketing investments.

Calculating the LTV per customer also allows a detailed analysis of the factors that contribute to greater profitability, such as the best products and the most appropriate communication channels. It is possible to determine the correlation between the price of the first purchase and the optimal profitability. In some industries, customers who spend more on the initial acquisition have the highest LTV. In other marketing categories, such as TV shopping, even the time of the commercial transaction can have a direct relationship on its level of return.[2]

Mapping the variables that influence the best purchasing responses provides valuable insight into the business, as well as into the most appropriate allocation of available resources. The often-used practice of heuristic marketing can be replaced by a systematic process of response analysis and investment concentration. A projection of the future customer base supported by LTV calculations helps companies better understand their main source of estimated income and allows them to redirect their activities toward the profitability axis. The qualitative concern for their buyer base takes priority over the quantitative aspects.

The Pareto Law

According to Newell,[3] there are two types of customers: the transactional and the relational. The former are interested in the best price, regardless of the brand. They are always in search of the best offer. For that precise reason, they generally provide relatively low rates of return for companies.

In contrast, relational customers seek trust, personalized services, and differentiated care. They do not mind paying more if it means saving time by not having to shop for other alternatives. They are more loyal, and they represent the company's best source of profitability. In many cases, they subsidize cheaper sales for the transactional segment.

The universe of profitable customers can be broken down into three categories: the highly profitable, which in general are relatively few in number, but represent the highest absolute profits for the company; those individuals who provide a healthy profit and have high potential for becoming members of the first segment; and, finally, those who provide marginal profit. By ranking the customers in order of importance and dividing them into five groups, it is possible to analyze the proportional contribution of each quintile to total profitability. In many businesses, it is possible to see that the profitability of each group is two or three times that of the following segment. The Pareto law was formulated by French engineer and mathematician Vilfredo Pareto, author of *Cours de l'Économie Politique*, who revolutionized the Lausanne School. The application of his book to marketing has been accepted around the world. It states that much of a brand's income or profit (typically 80 percent) is derived from a small portion of the customer base (typically 20 percent). This practical, universal rule demonstrates that in many cases it is possible to achieve high levels of efficiency through the directed allocation of resources. A few examples of categories that have accentuated the differences in profitability among their segments include the tourism and aviation industry, computer manufacturers, civil construction companies, car rental companies, beverage manufacturers, telecommunications companies, and banks.

Increasing a customer's LTV means extending his interaction cycle with the brand for as long as possible, while assuming that purchase frequency remains constant. Additional profits accrue, thanks to new transactions and new benefits resulting from the relationship. Customers refer other consumers and even help in product and service design, as we will see in detail in the next chapter.

To expand the period between each individual's first and last purchases, you need to develop relationship ties that make abandoning the brand more difficult. The more expensive it becomes to change to another supplier, the less chance there is that this will happen as a result of dissatisfaction with the brand, and consequently, the greater the chance of keeping the customer connected to the company. A rupture occurs precisely when there is an imbalance between the perceived values delivered by the company and the competition. Satisfaction and commitment result from perceived value. According to Heskett,[4] this measure is determined by the quotient of the results achieved from the purchase and the quality process, divided by the good's price and the costs incurred to acquire it:

$$\text{Perceived value} = \frac{\text{achieved results} + \text{quality process}}{\text{costs incurred} + \text{price}}$$

Levels of Customer Relationship with the Brand

There are many ways to maximize this equation. Using Gordon[5] as a reference, we can identify six main routes by which companies establish closer relationships with their customer base. In the structural connection, the company and the customer operate in an integrated manner, aligning their technology, people, and processes. For example, the integration between partners in the value chain, in the case of a relationship between companies, permits suppliers to update retail stocks automatically when the level reaches a critical value. For this to happen, it is necessary to build a strategic alignment between the companies, guaranteeing maximum quality in the process between those involved. As a consequence, the costs required to update or replace the merchandise on the shelves are reduced, resulting in increased value for the customer. The more complex the connection, the more costly it will be for the retailer to seek other suppliers. The time involved in locating a new company, helping it to assemble the required structure, and training it to use the process in the correct models is an enormous competitive differential for the existing supplier.

In the relationship between companies and consumers, the information systems for operational and financial control can become an instrument for additional value. For example, Federal Express provides systems that allow its users to track orders. The customers can locate their packages, thus reducing the chance of losses. Virtual bookstores, like Amazon, offer online statements for the latest purchases, which permit buyers to have easier control of their spending. Critical issues need to arise in order for there to be a rupture between the parties when there is a structural connection.

The second type of connection between customers and companies is based on brand value perception, established by the relationship with the brand's functional and emotional attributes. The stronger these attributes are, the greater the ties between the parties, resulting in additional perceived value in the purchase of products and services. If all other value delivery components are constant—for example, if two companies offer exactly the same products and services, with the same results and quality processes and identical price and access costs—then the consumer will choose the stronger brand. Exactly how to strengthen a brand is a topic that has been explored in several books. For more information, see Aaker[6] and Nilson.[7]

The attitudinal connection corresponds to ties established as a result of the company's professionalism. Its superior operational skills and unrelenting focus on the customer result in the delivery of a solution with high perceived value. Because it offers excellent products and services, a company with this type of connection may be able to charge prices that are higher than the competition's. Sony is an example of a company that uses this connection with its customers by means of a very objective set of values: outstanding technology and know-how sold to consumers who are able to pay for a differentiated solution.

The personal connection is characteristic of consultants, attorneys, and communication agencies. Company officers establish a link to the customers through personalized interaction and service. As a result, the barriers to breaking off a relationship become far higher. However, the company's dependence on specific people to attend to certain accounts also increases risks. When a professional changes companies, there is a chance that his or her clients will follow unless the company has developed relationship programs that explore how the customer interacts with the brand.

Companies can also increase their relationships with customers by adding value to each interaction. Point programs that reward users according to their interactions with the brand are prime examples of initiatives in this category. Airlines reward travelers according to miles flown, offering different discounts, special rest areas at airports, and promotions with other companies. As we will see in the next chapter, in this type of program, participants recognize the advantages through the available additional value, and in many cases, this may induce them to disregard the quality of some of the services being offered.

In special cases, there are companies with which customers are connected for reasons beyond their decision power. In regulatory environments, in which the government sets the rules for the relationship, or with monopolies, where individuals do not have the power of choice, perceived value can be quite low. The value equation introduced to compare diverse competitors becomes useless. In this situation, companies that do not develop a positive perception with their base, taking advantage of temporary favorable conditions, face a high rate of abandonment when the macroenvironment changes.

Marketing Investment Based on the Customer's LTV

Developing complete marketing programs based on the customer's LTV involves making the greatest investment in the portion of the base that has the highest value. The logic is simple: resources are scarce, and the best way to maximize the return on investment is by focusing on the best buyers. As a result, it is necessary to manage the relationship with each individual. Every interaction with customers in this category should be individual-ized, so that the marketing professional gains a sophisticated understanding of each customer. Using communication channels such as direct mail, telemarketing, and the Internet, the marketer must target with precision. The most valuable individuals receive the greatest percentage of the company's resources, time, and budget. Customer service centers are differentiated with respect to time and the technical expertise of service personnel. The Internet site provides a series of personalizations in restricted areas, and direct-mail pieces offer special prices and promotions. Each action should be carefully planned. The costs and the pur-chases made are mapped to the corresponding customers, per-mitting individual analysis of the return on the investments made.

The idea of maximizing return on investments doesn't apply to mass-marketing strategies and campaigns. In such cases, the marketing activities reach large numbers of people who may not even have the consumer profile for the products and services being offered. Niche marketing, on the other hand, is more focused on the target market, communicating the products and services that are consistent with that group's needs. However, it is unable to distinguish the most valuable customers from the rest of the base. Direct communication is the only way to reach the most valuable individuals in a personalized manner.

Regardless of the number of groups into which the customer base is divided, the main goal is to identify the different values that different customers bring and to develop the appropriate marketing programs. For the segments offering the greatest value, loyalty strategies should be created that will block the com-petition from gaining ground. For those customers with average profitability, cross-selling and product and service upgrades can result in increased sales and profitability. For the low-return group, in many cases, allocating more resources isn't like to pay off in improved profitability. So it makes sense to concentrate instead on investing in the select few who are most certain to provide greater returns. For companies whose base has wide disparities in value, incentive and point programs can become large competitive differentials. In the next chapter, we analyze relationship-marketing programs and their application to different user groups in detail.

Key Points

- Grouping consumers based on their needs is a common marketing practice. However, individuals with similar needs can provide different financial results for the brand. Therefore, it is essential to map out the most valuable consumers and create differentiated offers and services for them.
- In order to maximize the returns on marketing investments, companies use three main strategies: concentrate on the increase in sales volume, concentrate on the consumer's spending potential (share of pocket), or concentrate on the consumer's estimated monetary value throughout the period in which that customer generates income for the brand (lifetime value, or LTV).
- Calculating the LTV for each consumer permits a detailed analysis of the variables that contribute to greater profitability, such as the best products and the most appropriate communication channels.
- There are basically two kinds of consumers: the transactional and the relational. The former are interested in the best prices, regardless of brand, and generally provide very low rates of return for the company. The relational consumers seek trust, personalization of service, and differentiated care. They are more loyal and represent the company's greatest source of profitability.

- According to the Pareto law, the highest percentage of a brand's income or profit (typically 80 percent) is obtained from a small portion of the consumer base (typically 20 percent). This practical rule demonstrates that in many cases it is possible to achieve high levels of efficiency through the directed allocation of resources.
- To increase a consumer's LTV, expand the time during which the customer interacts with the brand to the longest period possible by encouraging purchases of new versions of already acquired products or additional categories of the same brand.

CHAPTER 3

Relationship Strategies to Win Over and Keep Customers

New customers historically signal growth and are still the main objective of marketers in the product and service industries. Whether by winning customers over from the competition or by penetrating new markets, high growth rates in the customer base inevitably reflect the focus and relevance of marketing investments.

On the other hand, the increasing concern with keeping consumers demonstrates the importance of paying attention to the brand's loyalty component. It is not enough to simply sell; marketers today must ensure that customers continue to feel that the brand brings value. A satisfied customer will buy new products or new versions that become available. By investing in customer retention programs, a company can increase its income without high acquisition expenses. The reason is simple: it costs several times more to attract a new customer than it does to keep an existing one.

Stages in the Brand-Customer Relationship

Achieving brand loyalty typically is a four-step process: awareness, consideration, conversion, and postsale. These stages represent the degree of the customer's proximity to the brand in relation to the exchange value.

In the first stage, the marketer's objective is to make the individual aware of the brand as a potential partner. The aim is to create a positive perception of the brand's reliability and quality in the consumer's mind so as to enable future communication.

It is in the consideration stage that the first contact between the company and the newly interested consumer occurs. To foster the possibility of a first purchase, the company must invest in the relationship. As a result, the marketing department must initiate a more personalized communication, introducing more detailed information about the brand and the products and services being sold. It is also important to show the connection between the price and what the product or service is offering. Although determining the price of the goods is not within the purview of the marketing communication department, establishing the link between the price and the product is one of the profession's most critical roles. When marketers make this argument effectively, it can advance (and help enhance) the relationship between the customer and the brand.

After this stage, it is natural for some individuals to lose interest in the products and services being offered. There are many reasons why this happens. After the initial contact with the brand, people may decide that the products or services are not of interest. Or, it could be that the marketing message during the consideration stage was inadequate and failed to present the necessary information. Sometimes other factors come into play: the price, distribution, or quality, for example, could fall short of what consumers desire.

But there will be consumers who show real interest, and it is imperative that they be engaged in a highly personalized manner. These people are truly interested in acquiring the product or service offered. For this reason, they are often called *prospects* or *hot leads*. Typically, they require minimal sales effort in order to be converted into customers, but they do require a specific, individualized response from the company. This can range from more proof of the efficacy of the product to financial incentives, including discounts or more payment options.

From the awareness to the conversion stage, the size of the base of potential customers will shrink dramatically as the process identifies those individuals who are truly interested in a value exchange with the brand. Marketers have to customize their message so that it has more depth and relevance to individual consumers. Relationship marketing uses the prospecting relationship marketing (PRM) program to develop these three initial stages and guarantee a systematic and structured process for acquiring new customers, as we will see in detail in this chapter.

Postsale is the final stage It comes after a sale has been achieved and reflects a mature—i.e., close—relationship with an existing customer. Although keeping current customers satisfied with a brand involves a great deal of work, it brings recompense to the company. Building loyalty is critical because often the costs incurred in bringing in new customers are considerable and are offset only when they make additional purchases.

The objective of a loyalty program, then, is to extend the living relationship between the company and its customers for as long as possible. As a result, it is necessary to rank customers in order of importance and develop corresponding marketing actions. Companies need to prioritize, devoting the most marketing efforts to those customer segments that offer the company the highest value. The various formats of segmentation will be explored in detail in Chapter 7.

There are loyalty programs that work on customer retention by focusing exclusively on identifying those individuals who are most likely to abandon the brand. In such cases, the marketers first try to understand what is driving customers to leave and then develop specific strategies to reverse this trend and communicate them clearly to this group. There can be many reasons for customers abandoning a brand, including dissatisfaction with support services or a better offer from the competition. What is key is that the company identify those individuals who are most at risk of leaving and then takes actions immediately to prevent their departure.

Recovery programs are used for customers who have already left the brand. Using statistical models for data analysis, companies can identify the most common reasons for leaving and then develop appropriate marketing campaigns to bring back the deserters. It is important to acknowledge that abandonment may not have anything to do with the company; it could be, for instance, that the customers have moved out of the state and no longer frequent that point of sale, or they may have experienced a dramatic decrease in disposable income.

The postsale stage offers tremendous opportunities. Satisfied customers trust the company and the brand enough to not only make repeat purchases when finishing products but also will acquire new versions and complementary solutions. In general, a product update provides some new benefit or additional features, while complementary solutions can satisfy a customer's need that hasn't been addressed by the existing product or service. Besides the immediate financial advantages from this practice, the company also gains increased customer loyalty. Customers who use a greater range of products and services from one company recognize that there are costs involved in searching for, analyzing, and buying a competing brand.

As described in Chapter 1, the customer's learning relationship with the brand is an additional barrier to abandonment that can be further reinforced by the sale of a broader set of solutions. Using a variety of techniques, relationship marketing employs cross-selling and upgraded programs and develops a consumption map of its customer base. It is thus possible to project customers' future consumption habits and then offer products and services geared to those customers at the time they are likely to be most in need of or wanting those items.

In addition to acquiring more goods and services from the company, the satisfied customer also can refer other potential buyers. This is so-called word-of-mouth marketing, which also is known as a member-get-member program in relationship-marketing circles. Here, the objective is to develop a targeted program, not simply to reap the benefits of a spontaneous phenomenon. The company uses its own loyal customer base as an inexpensive publicity arm by first identifying the biggest influencers among the base and then creating mechanisms that will facilitate their making a referral or indication. How to accomplish this? The key is building upon the pillars of recognition and reward.

First, the company needs to identify the customers who are seen as knowledgeable on the subject in question and who have the connections to disseminate the information. According to Gladwell,[1] what makes these people so influential is the fact that they know things that the rest of us do not. Then the company offers financial incentives to motivate these people to identify new potential customers. The reward could be a gift that is perceived as being of high value. In general, the greater the number of referrals made and turned into sales, the greater the rewards offered.

The difference between the member-get-member program and the PRM program is that in the former, the awareness stage is handled chiefly by individuals who already have some link (and thus credibility) with the consumer in question. Consequently, the leap to the final stages of the relationship can occur in a faster and more effective manner. In some industries, such as medical and hospital services, a referral from a reliable source is the determining factor in whether a consumer uses the offered solution.

The objective of relationship marketing programs is to move the customer straight to the most advanced stages of the relationship. For consumers who are unfamiliar with the company, the objective is to stir up brand awareness fast. For those who already know the company, the goal is to first take them to the consideration stage and then bring them to the conversion stage and make them customers. In the loyalty stage, the major challenge facing a company is to keep customers exercising their greatest purchase potential for as long as possible.

Figure 3.1 shows how the marketing professional can structure each of the described programs using the existing communication resources.

Figure 3.1 Relationship Stages with the Brand

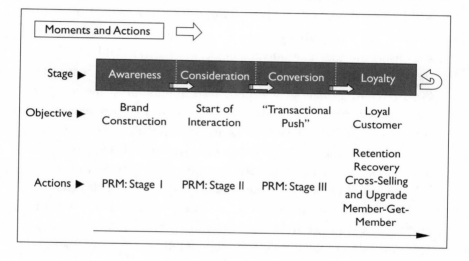

PRM—Prospecting Relationship Marketing

Until the 1960s, the public's buying patterns were more homogeneous and easily accessed, and the solution that mass marketers used to reach new consumers worked generally well. However, today there is an abundance of niche markets, each with its own unique demographic and behavioral characteristics, and as media costs continue to skyrocket, marketers need to make sure that their messages are appropriately tailored to the niche they seek to reach.

The biggest disadvantage of the mass media approach is that resources are being expended on reaching a segment of the customer base that may not have any interest in the product or service being offered. As John Wanamaker, the eponymous founder of the Wanamaker department store chain, supposedly quipped, "Half of everything I spend on advertising is lost; the problem is, I don't know which half." The pressure for greater returns on investment will force companies to increasingly supplement mass media strategy with a more efficient one.

Another prospecting possibility is to use several niche radio programs, magazines, and cable TV shows that target specific communities. Spreading communications over many smaller vehicles that are aimed at the special interests of small markets increases the marketing professional's chances of reaching the desired base effectively. This approach should also include renting lists that address specific communities, but in a direct manner. As we will see in Chapter 7, these lists can be commercialized by the vehicles themselves, associations or clubs, credit card companies, and public service companies, among others.

After identifying the best way to reach the target public and then employing that method of communication, the company needs to analyze the results of this action. If the outcome is positive—the number of prospects or customers reaches the projected quantity—then you can consider the strategy successful and keep using it until you notice the return rates begin to fall to unacceptable levels. It does not matter if there are individuals in this group who have already become customers or who have no interest at all in acquiring the products and services offered. The idea is to repeat the original message, or use a variation of it when necessary, so that a new crop of consumers becomes interested in the brand. Conversely, if the results from the initial media campaign are negative and far fewer customers result than expected, then look for other, more appropriate vehicles or lists. In both cases, the logic of the process assumes that the actions are completely independent of one another. They resemble a series of sporadic campaigns that do not use what was learned about individual behavior to refine future programs. There is no individualized management of the base to permit adjustments and improvements. The alternatives are concentrated in the search for new vehicles or lists and the creation of communication pieces. When these options run out, the company assumes that it has reached the inflection point for the product or service in question. Variables that are exogenous to marketing communication, such as the development of advanced versions of the solution or more competitive price policies, are used in an attempt to stave off the imagined end of the product's life cycle.

PRM's objective is to improve the return on investment in conquest marketing, preserving the history of contact with the base through communication management throughout the conversion cycle. It provides a systematic focus for acquisition marketing, with all actions developed with the base being carefully structured and related to one another. An attempt is made to improve and refine the relationship based on knowledge of the previous result. All answers are individually stored and updated.

PRM's strategy begins with the base's demographic and behavioral data. The relevant attributes of prospects are studied using descriptive analysis so that marketers can develop direct communications based on multiple factors. There also is an attempt to identify the groups that would find the brand most relevant and allocate communication resources accordingly.

Several companies make lists available for rental or purchase that provide information on consumer and company markets. In general, the data are comprehensive, covering the entire nation; they also are relevant, introducing a broad range of demographic, behavioral, and transactional attributes. Equally important, these lists are updated periodically, guaranteeing that the segmentation being used will classify the individuals correctly. An additional part of the potential customer base can also come from other contact lists that the company may have developed in the data-gathering process, such as at promotional events, points of sale, or Internet sites.

Once a list of prospects has been created, the company can make a range of brand communication channels available to the potential customer. A variety of channels will ensure that individuals will have the most convenient method at their disposal in order to develop the relationship.

PRM concentrates on differentiated procedures for each of the first three relationship stages: awareness, consideration, and conversion. In the first stage, most company efforts are aimed at making individuals aware of the brand and promoting a response. Direct mail, active telemarketing, and e-mails with links to the company's Web site are examples of direct communication methods that could be applied during this first stage. However, the database often lacks enough customer registrations to develop this campaign. In such cases, the media can be used as an additional tool to increase critical mass. It is important to observe that, contrary to conventional advertising's goal of brand building, relationship marketing's aim during this phase is to direct the consumers' response to specific contact points, such as phone service centers or Web sites (we will see more about this in Chapters 4 and 5).

The consideration stage involves a more directed handling of information. As a result of the initial communication, individuals now are interested in knowing more details. Internet sites are excellent channels for this purpose. With multimedia and interactivity capabilities, they can offer testimony from satisfied customers and details about products and services. Telephone service systems, points of sale for companies that wait on final consumers, and sales forces that service other companies (B2B) are other channels that can provide individualized treatment.

For the conversion stage, the relationship should be even more customized and the information provided even more targeted to the consumer. The use of personalization resources on the site permits the user to receive pages that are of interest immediately after being recognized, without having to navigate as in the previous stage. At the call center, the attendant recognizes the individual through the relationship history chart and goes more deeply into issues of greater relevance. The same thing happens at the point of sale or when the client is in contact with the sales force.

In all of these cases, it is important to record each individual's behavior activity and store the observed information in the databases:

- Which consumers are still in the initial stage and have not responded to communication actions?
- Which are in the consideration stage, and what is the most requested and sought-after information?
- Which are in the conversion stage, and what are the possible reasons that they have yet to migrate to the final postsale stage?

These data will be used to elaborate future, more refined strategies. Rather than discarding the portion of the base that did not become brand customers, the extension of the acquisition program will develop new direct actions called *rebounds*. The objective is to rewrite the communication by making an offer that is more directed toward the nonconverted base's objectives and needs during each of the awareness, consideration, and conversion stages.

With PRM, detailed communication planning should be implemented first, by specifying which actions should be developed in which channels and in which time unit. The results should be recorded and analyzed vis-à-vis the developed plan, and any discrepancies should result in the plan's being amended.

An initial objective is to use each channel in the most efficient manner possible, eliminating unnecessary costs in the contact phases. For example, use of the sales force is often one of the most expensive resources allocated. It should be employed only in advanced stages, when its presence can be a critical factor in the relationship's evolution. The primary objective is to convert the largest number of individuals into customers, using the method with the most advantageous cost-benefit ratio for the company.

Information on potential customers who have yet to decide on whether to buy the product or service is stored in the company database to be used for future programs. Current nonengagement does not justify removing these individuals from the prospect base. Companies should specify the consumers' reasons for reluctance or negativity so as to create strategies that will overcome those objections in the future.

Prospects that are already in advanced stages of the relationship should not receive communications as if they were unknown to the brand. Different people respond at different times. By understanding their behavior, it is possible to apply actions at the most opportune moments for each individual. By focusing on the prospect's perspective and using the PRM strategy, the marketing professional can attract new consumers in a more rational and intelligent manner. The key is enhancing both the content and the form of communications, rather than using homogeneous and uniform communications over and over again, thinking that the audience's behavior will somehow change by osmosis. Redirect the enormous media costs required by conventional prospecting into building more effective communication material and response channels. The database will then become a competitive differential. Unlike those vehicles that are available to any company that is willing to accept the costs involved, the prospect information bank is a comparative advantage that gives the brand a leg up on its competition. The prospect information bank is not reproducible, as every database is unique, nor can a structured PRM solution be bought or developed quickly. Like any learning process, it demands time. And in competitive industries, time is a resource that many companies do not have.

Member-Get-Member Programs

We all have a set of people to whom we relate. Relatives, friends, and work colleagues are just some of the ties we have made since our birth and throughout our social life. Unlike conventional approaches that use the list of potential customers as a reference, the member-get-member program explores the use of the existing ties between people as a channel to direct its messages. It is the vehicle that permits marketing communications to reach the desired prospect base. The process can be divided into five steps.

Step 1: Identify Those in the Customer Base Who Have Influencer Characteristics

In other words, identify the people who can influence your relationship group. These individuals will be responsible for initiating the awareness process, and, as Gladwell points out, the members of this group tend to have special characteristics. Some of them have the ability to connect to a large number of people, ensuring that the message reaches a broad base. The other group corresponds to the people who have a profound knowledge of the subject matter and whose opinions are therefore highly respected in their circle of contacts. And finally, there is a segment of influencers that is comfortable advocating and persuading others of its opinions.

The vast majority of company consumer databases typically do not have information regarding each person's degree of influence. That's why the first step is often to use the entire base as possible influencers. Note that by beginning the acquisition program with the existing customer base, the company eliminates one of the main problems found in the awareness stage: the high cost of media. Current customers are not important simply because they buy products and services. Because of the many connections they enjoy with other people, they also can be employed as inexpensive sales tools.

Step 2: Identify the Mechanisms That Encourage Customers to Use Their Influence with Their Network of Contacts

In general, the reasons for *indicating contacts* fit into two categories. The first one is related to the strong connection the customer has with the company. Brand advocates will defend and promote this relationship, extolling the benefits of the offered products and services throughout their communities. Customers who are impressed by a promotional offer or by another one of the solution's features can quickly inform their circle of contacts. The second reason is directly linked to the financial benefits that the influencer derives from the indication. For every new customer that this process brings in, the influencer receives a tangible benefit, which can be a discount toward the purchase of a new product, a special gift, or even monetary credit. The extent of this incentive is proportional to the effort the company desires from its influencers. Obviously, the greater the value, the greater the participants' effort will be.

Step 3: Identify the Best Mechanisms to Help Contact Groups Reach Other Segments, Which in Turn Will Influence Others, Who Will Influence Others, in an Endless Cycle

The strength of the member-get-member program is precisely that the process does not stop at the first level of customers within the company's base. It continuously extends outward, using the concept that those people who have been reached can influence their contact groups. The greater the number of levels, the more who will be influenced. The example shown in Godin[2] illustrates this scope. Let's begin with 10 individuals. Suppose that each influenced person reaches 5 more. Of these 5, only half remain interested and influence their contact base. If this process occurs in 18 successive repetitions, 58 million people will be reached! Although this example is not derived from a real case, it demonstrates mathematically the dimensions that a well-developed program of this kind can assume.

Step 4: Create the Communication with an Appropriate Message, Develop Tools That Facilitate the Indication of New People, and Begin the Program

Personal communication with customers can be handled by direct mail, e-mail marketing, or telemarketing. A Web site with more detailed information about the program can be developed. At the first level, the message should reach those customers with whom the company has permission to interact. Besides the main content, which may be associated with the sale of some product, a promotion, or a description of some special features of the item, the communication must contain clear rules concerning the awards that can be won by referring new customers.

The company can create tools that facilitate spreading the message to others. For this aspect of the program, the Internet is the fastest channel for reaching large groups of people. An e-mail with fields to indicate those who may be interested or a site that offers a discount if you provide the e-mail addresses of other interested customers permits the spreading of member-get-member programs with a few clicks.

The same site that shows details of the program can be used by participants to check the number of successful referrals and choose the available awards associated with their scores. Although those who don't have Internet access can get this information through monthly statements sent by snail mail or from phone centers, the clear superiority of digital media in terms of speed and cost sometimes justifies the suppression of these other channels.

Step 5: Analyze the Results and Refine Future Actions

It is essential to store the information on the program in the database:

- Which people gave the most referrals?
- Which referrals generated new customers?
- What is the communication's average response time?
- How many levels did the program reach?
- What is the relationship tree among the participants?

The data should be analyzed to determine the results of the program and refine the existing initial information about the customer base. The database can be augmented with behavioral information, highlighting the best influencers, their relationship group, and how they respond to the offers. This will permit the elaboration of more precise future actions with more advantageous return on investment rates.

Some companies have used acquisition programs based on word-of-mouth or click-to-click communication to increase sales. Amazon, the virtual bookstore, has affiliate programs for people who are interested in earning a sales percentage from its products. These people include links to the virtual store's address on their sites. When visitors from these sites purchase products from Amazon, the corresponding credit is automatically made available.

Other companies use the network or multilevel sales concept as a business model. These are not merely communication strategies to increase their customer base but the main business process that will expand market capabilities and product distribution. Amway, Primerica, Nuskin, and Herbalife are some examples of companies that earn millions of dollars per year basing their business strategies on the member-get-member model.

Loyalty

Many companies' primary growth strategy is still to invest heavily in the acquisition of new customers. After all, if the number of new customers, or conquests, increases every year, the financial results should head in the same direction, right? Wrong! New customers do not necessarily mean that the company is in a growth process. If the existing customers start to abandon the brand, simple math shows that the total number could decrease. If the spending volume of those who migrate to the competition's products and services is greater than the amount of spending by new customers, the final result will be a drop in earnings. Investments in acquisition programs end up being rendered useless by abandonment rates among existing customers.

Take AOL's strategy in Latin America. It used a massive advertising campaign and free distribution of CDs, despite the heavy costs, according to the *Wall Street Journal*.[3] Although it gathered 1.3 million users during its three years of operations, more than 100,000 of those subscribers did not pay their bills and were subsequently disconnected from the provider. The results were operational losses that left AOL in an extremely precarious situation in the region. The company's financial director considered abandoning the Latin American market entirely if this was not turned around. Eventually, that is what actually happened.

The objective of a loyalty program is to keep customers satisfied, eliminating consideration of the competitor's alternative.

The mechanism employed is to provide individuals with reasons to remain loyal by establishing ties that will rarely be copied by other companies.

Loyalty's financial dimension works with the price variable, providing bigger discounts for greater purchase volumes or increasing the number of installments to pay for the merchandise. It can also explore the reward aspect for the most loyal customers. In these award programs, customers accumulate points that can be exchanged for prizes. The points are related to activities that the company wants the customer to carry out, such as buying new products, visiting points of sale for experimentation, or navigating on the site to get to know new pages. The available awards can vary from discounts on the purchase of new merchandise to fun incentives like trips, cars, and electronic devices. The airlines' mileage programs are examples of awards associated with the number of miles flown. When the user begins to accumulate points and take advantage of free trips, the choice of the transporter is reinforced, regardless of the quality of its product and service.

The mechanism that puts these programs into operation involves sending a personalized card with a unique identifier to each participant. The participant uses the individualized code with activities that credit points. A database is used to store the information from each of the participants and that participant's accumulated point total. With the stored information, the company can develop direct communication actions by means of direct mail, e-mail marketing, or telemarketing, encouraging increased use. There may be a Web site available to accompany the account status, thus ensuring process transparency.

Loyalty explores other components besides the financial to keep customers satisfied. Some of these, such as product and service quality and value delivery infrastructure, do not depend on marketing communication. Customization, convenience, brand perception, creation of communities, and cross-selling, on the other hand, are variables that can be explored by relationship marketing to guarantee that the company will have a closer relationship with its base, as we shall see further ahead.

Customization

Customization is the capacity to communicate with the customer in an individualized manner, as opposed to a one-size-fits-all approach that deals with all people in the same way. Customers have different interests, values, and purchasing habits and should therefore be treated differently.

In the beginning of the last century, when stores served only a few dozen people, customization was guaranteed. But today, when companies have tens or even hundreds of thousands of customers, providing personalized service is more challenging. Technology can be helpful in this regard, supporting the construction of large user databases and customizing the content and form used in on- and offline relationship channels.[4] Computers can print out direct-mail pieces with different information for each segment of the customer base. Web sites and personalized e-mails permit a completely individualized interaction, sending each Internet user a message that is in accord with his or her interests.

Convenience

It is possible to make the customer base's relationship with the company easy by identifying the individuals and their histories and providing optimized resources that enable them to interact with the brand. Some convenient solutions include making bank statements available through home banking, reducing the response time at phone service centers by using prepared scripts, and providing support so that customers can locate products at the point of sale.

The Internet channel has a series of tools that facilitate interaction with the Internet user. ClickToChat is a solution that permits a chat window to open in the user's browser where it is possible to pose questions to an assistant in real time. ClickToCall, meanwhile, asks the attendant to get in phone contact without the user stopping navigation. (It is assumed that the user has at least two phone lines available.) ClickToTalk provides the same function over a VoIP (voice over Internet Protocol) channel. The ClickToSync tool allows the attendant to literally take control of the user's browser, guiding him or her to the appropriate page where answers to the most important questions can be found. With increasingly large Web sites, these tools serve an important function, helping the Internet user to locate the desired information in a quick and simple manner.

At the point of sale, the combination of multimedia displays with the use of personalized human service can make purchases easier and more convenient. These displays, or electronic kiosks, as they are also known, show detailed information on the available products and permit price reading with bar code scanners when the products are small. Office Depot, one of the largest office supply retailers in the United States, equipped its point-of-sale attendants with handhelds connected to remote servers that provide dynamic information about the company's product line. When a buyer asks a question about an item's technical advantages or the best way to use it, the attendants can easily find the answers. It is a way to add value not only to the purchase but to the entire relationship, offering services that strengthen the customer's interaction with the company.

Telephone service centers are another contact point where the user can get customer support or get information about a new product. This service must be fast both in serving callers and in solving problems. Being put on hold for a long time before having someone finally answer has been one of the biggest consumer complaints. Audible response units (ARUs), which are available to automate this interaction, respond in part to those questions.

Because of the high costs involved in maintaining a channel like this with a large number of attendants, companies try to strike a balance between technological and human resources.

Although some people use a single channel to interact with the company, the most common model involves a combination of channels. For example, a user can request a catalog by mail, use the Internet to learn more details about a specific product, make the purchase at a point of sale, and use phone support for any doubts regarding the product's use. It is fundamental to provide access to all channels that consumers could desire. Each customer's register must contain complete information, regardless of the channel being used at the moment, in order to provide the most convenient service possible.

Brand Perception

The chances of keeping a customer loyal to a brand increase in proportion to the customer's satisfaction with the company. Although strengthening a brand involves a range of issues that go beyond the scope of this book, it is important to underscore the principle that relationship marketing seeks to ensure a positive perception of the brand through systematic communication with the customer base, which in turn influences the outcome of the relationship.

Some examples of relationship-strengthening actions include sending birthday greetings and holiday wishes for Christmas and New Year's; sending a welcome kit or material congratulating the person who has just become a customer; sending a notice of an anniversary of the account; sending periodic newsletters with information about products, the company, the market, and the latest news; inviting the customers to attend events, training, and workshops; sending bulletins whenever something important happens, such as a product recall; and e-mailing confirmations of purchases of merchandise from a virtual store.

Creation of Communities

It's often assumed that marketing messages should emanate from the company and go to the consumer. But in the section on member-get-member campaigns, we saw that there is another alternative in which the individual customer redirects communications to other people in the relationship chain. Communities or loyalty clubs are another option for marketing programs that explore this concept. They promote a high degree of participation and commitment on the part of those involved. They are generally created by the company with the objective of strengthening the relationship with one or more segments of the base. Not all customers need to be engaged in these programs.

Some forms of interaction can take place through discussion forums to exchange information, online events with professionals in chat rooms, sponsoring of offline events to meet people, and the creation of e-mail lists that can be shared among members.

The company strengthens the relationship with the participants by sponsoring a unique experience for all, thus demonstrating its dedication to them and its commitment to building trust. The communication becomes more customized, since tracking the group permits a greater understanding of the base's behavioral characteristics, which allows for a more precise segmentation.

Interaction between the involved parties enables the company to address doubts about the use of the products or services it offers. This makes customer service both more convenient and more complete.

When customers have greater involvement with the company, that also facilitates the generation of new ideas and identifies problems when fixes are still possible. Procter & Gamble developed a solution a few years age that permits customers to talk and give opinions about the company's products on its site. First, the individual is invited to become part of the group, and he or she registers to participate. From that point on, the person becomes a brand collaborator and can give opinions and comments and ask questions on company-related issues. The person can check how his or her ideas are being accepted by the group. Participants will be e-mailed answers to their questions, and they will be directed to exclusive registration areas on the site. Using an administrative tool, the company can control program development with statistics and analyses in real time.

However, if those communities play an important role in strengthening the company's relationship with its base, implementing them also requires a great deal of care. They should never be abandoned during the early stages because they are mid- and long-term solutions. Because they permit customers to get to know one another and openly exchange information with one another, it is fundamental for the relationship with the base to be transparent and without conflicts. A disgruntled individual could affect the dynamics in a large group.

More recently, the rise of virtual communities supported by the Internet has attracted tens of millions of people. These ones have completely different dynamics compared to the communities created by companies. See Chapter 4 for more information on the most advanced stages in the creation of communities.

Cross-Selling and Upgrades

Those customers who have the strongest relationships with the company also have the greatest likelihood of purchasing the broadest range of products and services. Those who are satisfied with a TV that they purchased will choose a DVD of the same brand, and most probably a sound system and portable music player as well. Cross-selling is the process of selling products or services in a different category, although related to previously purchased merchandise.

An upgrade is the sale of an updated version of an already owned product. Those who are satisfied with the purchase of an automobile but want to acquire a new model will look for a newer option from the same manufacturer. A person who now wants a faster version of his old computer will consider the same manufacturer's alternative first. The same occurs for other business categories as well, whether foods, clothing, household appliances, services for final users, or services between companies.

Cross-selling and upgrades can become a great source of income for companies. With propensity models for products and services, it is possible to plot the customer segments with the greatest potential for purchases in specific categories and in a particular time unit. It is thus possible to use direct communication through e-mail marketing, direct mail, or telemarketing to offer the most appropriate solution at the most appropriate time.

Loyalty indicators improve when the customer spends more money on a wider range of brand products. According to Newell,[5] banks keep those clients with whom they have multiple sales relationships three to four times longer than those with whom they have a single relationship. It is generally easier and cheaper to expand the offering of products and services for the current customer base than it is to attract new buyers. Cross-selling and upgrades increase income by combining sales increases with customer base loyalty.

Retention and Recovery

Small reductions in abandonment rates for profitable customers can correspond to large increases in company profits. Studies show that in some cases, a 5 percent increase in retention rates can mean growth in returns of anywhere from 40 to 95 percent.[6]

It is necessary to accept the fact that customers have an average relationship period with the brand, after which they begin to abandon it. This can occur for reasons that are either intrinsic or completely unrelated to company operations. Dissatisfaction with the product, service, or support may lead customers to abandon a brand, but it's also possible that a change in the customers' behavioral or demographic profile, such as a new address, aging, or altered consumption habits, was the cause. The objective of retention and recovery programs is to systematically identify the main causes of dissatisfaction and avoid having groups or segments move away from the company prematurely, or recover them if they have already migrated to the competition.

According to Hansotia,[7] there are eight steps that the company must take to create these programs:

Step 1: Segment the base, ranking the groups according to their different relationship intensities with the brand.

Step 2: Identify the most important groups that should be focused on first. Those who buy more and who have the greatest potential for abandonment should be the top priority.

Step 3: For each group, analyze the typical behavior during the latency period, which corresponds to the interval between two consecutive purchases. Identify the members of this group who behave differently and interact less with the brand.

Step 4: Try to find the main reasons that these members behave this way, using focus group studies whenever necessary.

Step 5: Neutralize the reasons for abandonment whenever possible.

Step 6: Communicate the new procedures to group members in a direct and personalized manner, demonstrating the company's concern for them.

Step 7: Evaluate the financial performance of the implemented changes.

Step 8: Write the success models that permit associating
   customers with the most appropriate retention and recovery
   programs to justify marketing investments in this area.

Marketing professionals are increasingly using direct channels
of communication to reach their customers. Unlike mass communication solutions, these channels permit greater control, in
content as well as circulation, over a medium with smaller penetration or market coverage. The message can be more comprehensive, the formats more varied, and the text more directed to
company interests. The number of customers affected by the
message can vary depending on the planned budget.

As we saw in the previous chapter, purchase volume in a specific
period of time varies from person to person. The Pareto law
describes the pattern in many business categories in which a small
percentage of customers is responsible for a large part of company
income. Identifying the best allocation of communication resources
is equivalent to providing the solutions with the greatest value to
the most valuable clients for the brand. Rather than treat the entire
customer base in a homogeneous manner, the marketing professional should break the base down into different segments and give
the most attention to the most important groups.

Key Points

- The historical objective of product and service industries has
  been to attract new consumers. Only recently has there been
  increasing concern with retaining individuals of greater value.
  Relationship marketing uses specific programs for acquiring
  and retaining consumers based on the stage of the target
  public's relationship with the brand. There are typically four
  relationship stages: awareness, consideration, conversion, and

loyalty. In the first, the objective of a marketing action is to make the individual aware that the company can be its partner in an exchange of value. The consideration stage establishes the first contact between the two parties, presenting more information about the brand and its products and services. In the conversion stage, those individuals who show real interest, called prospects or hot leads, generally require a small sales effort if they are to become, or to be converted into, consumers of the brand. At this stage, all that is required may be providing a customized response to specific questions or perhaps some financial incentives, such as discounts or a broader range of payment plans. From the awareness to the conversion stage, the size of the original base gets smaller because of the refining process, which results in the identification of truly interested individuals.

- Relationship marketing uses the PRM (prospecting relationship marketing) program to develop these first three stages and guarantee a systemic and structured process for acquiring new consumers. The most advanced stage is the loyalty stage, and it corresponds to the relationship with the existing consumer base. If the consumer is satisfied, he or she trusts the company and becomes a repeat customer, buying new products and services from the company when the existing ones need to be replaced; the consumer will also acquire new versions and complementary solutions. Even more important, the consumer can refer other potential buyers. In relationship marketing, this is called a member-get-member program, which explores the existing ties between people to win over new consumers.

- The objective of a loyalty program is to extend this relationship between the company and its customers for as long as possible. The strategy is to provide the individual with enough reasons to keep him or her loyal, establishing ties that will be hard for other companies to duplicate. Loyalty programs can explore the financial aspect by offering discounts or award programs for the most loyal customers.

- Other variables that can be used to guarantee a more intimate relationship with the customer base include customization, convenience, brand perception, creation of communities, cross-selling, and upgrades. The objective of retention and recovery programs is to systematically identify the main causes of customer dissatisfaction, avoid having some groups or segments leave the company before the appropriate moment, and recover those who may have left for the competition.

The New Integrated Communication Scenario Based on Relationship-Marketing Strategies

Integrated brand communications has become the topic du jour in daily meetings, college marketing classes, and corporate seminars. In an increasingly cluttered media environment, marketing professionals face the daunting challenge of linking all the disparate communication activities by various specialized agencies on behalf of the brand. In this chapter, we will explain how and why this integration—shaped by relationship-marketing managers—is the most modern and profitable way to guarantee a relevant, unified message, with high returns for the brand. We will also reveal the leading role that relationship-marketing strategy can play in integrated communications, ensuring that all communication agents are in sync and serving the consumer.

It is already well known that there are a variety of ways in which a brand can reach the target public, especially since consumers now demand a plethora of channels through which to interact with brands. Companies that want to strengthen their relationship with their customer base have many avenues available to them, such as fairs and splashy promotional events, the Internet, points of sale, and customer service centers, to name just a few. Being absent from any of these venues could mean the loss of new sales or even neglecting a huge swath of the target public. The retail store that simply opens its doors at 8 a.m., waits for clients to stream in, then closes at 7 p.m. is confronting a new reality in the Internet age. Buyers are no longer limited by geography or time, since it is possible for them to shop and spend via telephone or high-speed cables whenever and wherever they choose.

Filling in all the communication gaps can become a great challenge, especially when companies understand that all channels should be integrated. This is not merely about applying a good media mix. Being present at several contact points requires that the various communication channels present a clear message that is consistent with the way the brand has been positioned. The idea is that the target consumers will eventually get to know the company through these various and coherent messages being directed at them.

Integration of Direct and Mass Communication

Even if marketing communication is plural, ideally, the message should be singular. A brand, product, and marketing campaign that seek high returns must be aimed at the full range of the target consumers' way of life. In other words, such a campaign should address each person's primary or primal habits, values, and principles.

In multimedia campaigns, where consumers can see the same brand represented on TV and radio, in newspapers, on the Internet, through direct mail, at the point of sale, and in countless other media, it's essential that the message be in horizontal harmony. Ideally, concepts, texts, and images must be unified, each reinforcing the others and providing the consumer with a unique impression of the brand. Vertical harmony, on the other hand, seeks interconnected communication channels that are sequential and complementary. This means that when one communication channel goes off the air, another takes its place. It is thus possible to keep the brand constantly present in an annual campaign, not necessarily by using several different communication vehicles at the same time, but by using each one of them for a certain period of time only.

Integrated communication is based on the strategic orchestration of existing actions. But this is not merely a temporal issue, as has been the case in the past. Communication initiatives must be planned for the different channels in order to guarantee that the correct content and form are employed. Synchronized planning becomes even more imperative with the proliferation of brands, products and services, communication channels, and marketing programs for different consumer segments offered by companies. A marketing plan's final result will be measured not by the sum of all the messages directed to the target public, but by the cumulative impact of several actions. This is the so-called virtuous effect, in which every additional message complements the one before it, adding value precisely because it gives the consumer the correct image at the correct time and in the correct form.

In many cases, the addition of unplanned complementary actions to increase contact with the target public can actually nullify the positive effects generated by the previous messages. This happens when the new information is at odds with consumer expectations. In this situation, additional investments have negative returns and can compromise the success of the entire campaign. It is possible to maximize the return on investment only with the precise and careful application of each component of the communication mix.

It is worth noting that while the implementation of a specific action can be dealt with tactically, the adoption of integrated communication is directly linked to the strategic field of action. Thus, the repertoire of messages directed to the target public has two objectives. One is short term and aimed at maximizing the return on investment for each individual action. The other is more long range and is analyzed more in terms of its impact on business objectives and company marketing goals.

Integrated communication generally requires the participation of several vendors, like direct marketing, advertising, public relations, and Web marketing agencies. Regardless of each communication action's individual results, an integrated vision is generally required in order to manage all efforts. For any brand that wants to develop a message with impact, the challenge is to ensure that all the participants' goals are aligned. This is possible when the individual consumer is at the center of all marketing decisions. Then, the main objective becomes making sure that the individual's evolution follows the relationship curve with the brand. As soon as the channel's tactical maneuvers take a secondary role, the main goal becomes creating integration.

The starting point for developing integrated communication action is to recognize that the target public has a dynamic and multifaceted profile. These people have different jobs, lifestyles, and zip codes. As a result, it is necessary to segment consumers based on marketing objectives. You must employ the most appropriate channels for each group in a complementary manner.

Internet and direct marketing already rely on individualized communication to maximize results. Because of the very nature of those platforms, each consumer can receive a customized message, and the responses from consumers can also be followed one by one. Advertising, promotion, and public relations, in contrast, are based on mass media platforms, which, by definition, require uniform treatment of large numbers of people. However, these vehicles can be included in integrated communication programs. They simply need to be planned and coordinated from a relationship-marketing perspective, rather than as independent communication solutions. But how is that possible when the individuals receiving the mass communication are not identifiable? The answer lies in redesigning the main objectives of each action. Thus, rather than trying to reach the maximum number of people, seek instead to provoke some kind of response from individual consumers. Through this strategy, known as a call to action, individuals will be identified as they announce their intentions to the company. And from that moment on, marketers can track the individuals' relationship with the brand and develop programs on other channels that facilitate direct communication. When you waste such opportunities to differentiate the users of mass media, you will not be able to distinguish the prospects from those who showed no interest in your offer. The result is that you repeat the same message, over and over again, to the entire base, with little success. The call-to-action technique, along with registering each individual, allows mass media platforms to be integrated into a customized communication repertoire.

This change in attitude can have a striking impact on the returns of marketing programs. According to Roman,[1] when multiple media are employed in a precise manner, the results generate qualified double-digit responses. Measurements made over several years have shown a corresponding increase in consumer satisfaction and LTV.

Communication Actions Integrated by Relationships

Marketing professionals can tap a wide range of actions for everyday functions. When each action is based on relationship-marketing strategies, the returns can be measured and the results continuously improved. Some of these long-standing communication actions will now be analyzed from this perspective. The goal is not to list all the possibilities or describe them in detail, but to show how a shift in the approach to conventional practices can result in what we argue is the accurate application of integrated communications. We do not limit our discussion to communication actions directed at the consumer market. We also cover communications aimed at trade and retail segments and at corporate partners. Collectively, they create synergy and maximize solutions.

Endomarketing: Integration Begins with the Employees

The launching of new products and campaigns begins with the company's team. This is called business-to-employee communication, or B2E. Keeping employees informed and in sync with corporate strategy is no simple task. Therefore, this is the ideal starting point for integrated communication.

According to answers to marketing tests, the campaigns that achieve the best results typically begin inside a company. When human resource, marketing, and finance professionals conduct B2E campaigns, they usually carry out the task right in front of their own teams, which has been a great limiting factor in terms of covering broad geographic areas. This method makes fulfilling the many other company demands even more difficult.

But in the 1990s, with the development of new computer technology, an internal network of tools called an intranet was created, and this is a powerful source of managerial, financial, and operational information. Using these tools, communication professionals can fulfill their mission to disseminate marketing's latest decisions, whether that means information about the launching of new products, the opening of new markets, or simply brand performance. Thus, by making communicating to the advertiser's internal staff a high priority, the professional gets valuable practice, which helps guarantee good results later.

Trade Marketing: Involving the Resellers

To guarantee successful results in consumer goods or industry campaigns, it's essential to integrate communications with the point-of-sale (POS) network, preparing distributors, resellers, and representatives before launching the product. The channels that form the product distribution chain in traditional retail are still business's great intermediary between industry and the consumer market.

For many decades, whenever new products were launched, it was the company's sales force that would take the idea for a particular campaign to the POS. The broadside is a classical piece.[2] It is an exclusive pamphlet for the channel that summarizes the creation and all media that will be used to generate sales turnover and attract consumers to stores.

Now, with the Internet and an integrated approach, the broadside is electronic and has the additional advantage of being able to accompany a sequential and creative marketing campaign. An exclusive business-to-business (B2B) site is created for the relationship with resellers. In this new scenario, the limitations and costs of paper don't exist; and it's quick and easy to update the campaign. An electronics manufacturer, for example, could create an extranet that is linked to the POS, so that the company can inform people about new launches and train sales staff through a virtual school. An extranet is also an excellent way to promote and manage incentive campaigns.

Promotion: Short- and Long-Term Gains

Since promotion is a strong engine for driving sales and bringing immediate returns, it is always assured a place in a campaign. The basic model consists of an annual promotional calendar that creates extra incentives by taking advantage of special dates as part of a plan to increase demand for the brand.

When this is incorporated into the relationship strategy, the first task should be to classify the target consumers into groups, based on their current or future value to the company. From this perspective, the temporary nature of a specific brand's promotion is exceeded. For example, in a neighborhood-to-neighborhood promotion effort, the promoters are trained to amass a database from visits to homes; as well as making sales, they are supposed to write down the reasons why consumers did not make a purchase. What in the past was simply a lost sale, today is another registered consumer for another possible sale in the future. A marketer who is schooled in relationship marketing can glean the target public's demographic and behavioral information. For example, when a consumer says, "No, thank you; I'm not interested now," he or she may add, if asked, that he or she would very much like to buy the product, but cannot do so right now because there are still three installments to be paid on some other merchandise. By qualifying this negative and using relationship marketing as a tool, this same consumer can be contacted three months from now, when the last installment will be paid off. Promotion is thus given additional strength, improving its reply rates when strategically tied to the relationship.

Advertising Integrated by a Relationship Strategy: A Combination of Verifiable Results

Everyone knows that advertising is the pioneer discipline, the mother of marketing communication. Its power of persuasion builds companies, products, political leaders, and, more recently, even new religions that penetrate the mass media. When evaluated at its core, advertising can be reduced to three key points: it has quick and comprehensive coverage, it saturates diverse socioeconomic strata, and it is able to instill new attitudes through its creative power.

To integrate advertising means to add the best of two worlds. Advertising's broad-based coverage and impact are added to the creative call-to-action technique, with its telephone (1-800) and Internet (www.com site) operations plus the offers to encourage replies. With this mix, used as a relationship tool, traditional advertising is called direct-response advertising (DRA) and takes on a form and content different from those of the traditional ad. Rapp Collins calls it double-duty advertising. It paints a more complete picture in text and images, describing in detail the product's benefits, its price, and the means of payment that are available—all the while encouraging the consumer to give a positive response. Thus, while advertising influences attitudes, good reply campaigns stir up consumer behavior, leading to a call to action or the beginning of a dialogue. Another important differential offered by double-duty advertising is the creative strategy that guarantees simultaneously sales, the building of a brand, and the creation of a residual database to provide continuity to the campaign through direct relationship actions. The advertiser's budget is thus optimized, satisfying several objectives with a single media investment.

All this synergy and integration reaches its climax when the advertiser is shown the return on investment (ROI) calculation. This is possible only here, and not with traditional advertising, thanks to DRA's resources that monitor and measure the campaign response volume.

Direct Mail: Why Integration Is Worthwhile

When direct-mail actions are integrated with other communications actions, such as advertising, there is a marked improvement in result rates. Therefore, integration is recommended. If direct mail is used in an isolated fashion, with strong personalization and a pertinent offer, it can generate good response levels. However, the results will always be inferior to those achieved when there is a creative and sequential combination of direct mail and other brand communication actions.

The large brands that lead their product and service categories are already working at integrating their communication with synchronized direct-mail actions. Here, layout solutions can incorporate creative themes and personalities (photos) from the communication campaign. On the other hand, chronological synergy creates a simultaneous or sequential triggering of mailings according to the mass media plan. The latest results obtained prove that this is one of the best marketing models.

Events: How to Prolong Their Impact

Events are, by their nature, bold, and thus are ideal for product launches. An event seeks to assemble the most influential primary and secondary members of the public at a single place and time. It needs many components to be successful. Its planning, creation, and execution must be impeccable. It is also critical to bring and charm the right guests on the right day and at the precise time. There is no room for correction later. The public normally comes and goes in large numbers, and people are under the effect of the sponsoring brand only while the show lasts.

With integration guided by the relationship strategy, planning begins much earlier than is the norm. For trade industry events, the guest list must be chosen with great care; the value of each guest can be reduced to a mathematical calculation based on each person's financial history with the brand. At times, this can transcend personal preferences. However, in events aimed at the general public, such as large music shows sponsored by specific brands, many tasks can be handled while the event is in progress. It is very common to use short questionnaires or quick interviews to gather more data and flesh out the profile of the attendees. Thus, after the event, the brand can continue its relationship with that public, establishing personalized relationship links and prolonging contact with those groups that hold real value for the brand.

Large events can represent excellent opportunities to gather data. Thus, after the emphasis given to the promotion of the show in newspapers, magazines, and electronic media, an additional value is sought by retaining information on that public in a database for continuous relationship actions. The plan is for the brands to take advantage of this unique occasion to develop a more complete picture of the contact base and develop direct communication programs after the event, ensuring more effective results for this type of action.

Public Relations: Improving Segmentation

Public relations is an old, subtle, and strong ally of marketing communications that is appropriate for influencing select segments of the public. Closely related to the press, public relations often makes good use of these ties to shape opinion.

The very nature of its work, which is geared toward winning specific public spheres, requires identifying and focusing on the most essential segments of the customer base. For this, building a database is highly recommended. Since this task traditionally involves face-to-face contact, personal phone calls, and events to develop a network of relationships and influences, it fits well with relationship marketing's typical one-on-one relationship strategy. In public relations work, integration can extend and multiply the possibilities of achieving contact with those sought-after individuals. With tools such as direct mail or the Internet, personalized and frequent messages can efficiently fill in the inevitable gaps when personal contact is not possible. Special

steps may be necessary when reaching out to journalists, especially if the goal is to arouse reporters' interest and guarantee
their attendance at key press conferences.

Relationship strategies can dramatically enhance the geographic reach of public relations work, thus reducing its costs
and increasing its effectiveness by giving brands broad national
coverage. Still more important, it can maintain scrupulous
records of the success and limitations of each relationship, and
build a special database that details the history of contacts with
each influential person and their contributions. This material can
help optimize results by guiding future decisions about new
investments in this same customer base.

The Internet: The Revolution in Relationships with the Consumer

When it comes to reaching individuals, the Internet is the most
powerful interactive communications tool. It permits the naviga-
tor a broad interactive experience with digital resources. Conventional TV turns into interactive TV, radio into interactive
radio, direct mail into e-mail, telemarketing into voice over Internet Protocol (VoIP), and printed material into electronic content
(see Figure 4.1).

For the consumer, the Internet offers the possibility of interacting to a degree never before imagined. First, users can navigate within a message, selectively delving deeper into topics that
are of greater interest to them and discarding things that they
consider unimportant. Second, traditional unidirectional communication emanating from the company to its base is transformed into a two-way channel. The Internet provides resources
so that the user now can ask a question to the company, and dig
deeper on the feedback.

Figure 4.1 The Internet's Role in Marketing

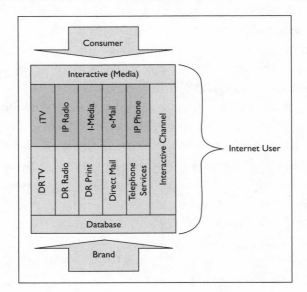

For corporations, the impact of using the Internet has also been quite profound. Now, organizations must be structured in a way that fosters dialogue with the customer base. That requires agility. It is useless to answer a customer's e-mail a few days after it was sent. To ensure individualized interaction, corporations also need to personalize communications. Marketing strategy results will be meaningful for brands that take advantage of the new capabilities of the interactive media, treating them as opportunities to build a database for Internet users and create closer relationships with them.

The advantages of online relationships reflect the rapid inroads that this channel has made in response to market needs. In its initial phase, the Internet was characterized by static, generally corporate-looking pages that introduced the company and its products. The content was the same for all interested parties, and the main concern was making basic information available. In the next phase, corporate Web sites became more personalized, offering dynamic content for the user. Financial transactions, or e-commerce, emerged. The user was able to make purchases over the Internet, and the system personalized sales offers according to each customer's area of interest.

In its third stage, the Internet recognizes users individually and customizes solutions accordingly. The customer's relationship with the brand is vigorously managed, always with an eye to taking it to a higher level. Automatic responses and personalized solutions are applied to establish dialogue with the Internet users and ensure that their expectations are satisfied. Interactive channels are not limited to PCs. Different devices, with other capacities and access speeds, are also supported. This is called a convergence continuum (see Figure 4.2). Personal computers with dial-up or broadband lines, interactive TVs and game consoles, handhelds, PDAs, cell phones, and even systems embedded in everyday machines like refrigerators and cars can be directly connected to the network. It is this vast range of options that has created such vast relationship opportunities.

Figure 4.2 The Convergence Continuum

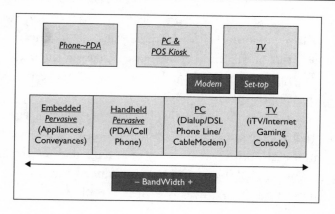

In its most advanced stage, the Internet provides a connection among people on a unique scale. This is how organized groups of individuals that divide and share information and similar interests are consolidated.

Known as social relationship networks, these virtual spaces allow the exchange of ideas and impressions about the most varied themes, such as religion, soccer, companies, products, tourism, arts, and the economy. The participants in these networks exchange opinions, links, audio and video files, photos, and other forms of content.

In this space, messages are quickly spread among the members, the individuals commit themselves to never sending advertisements or other forms of spam to the rest of the group, and the control of the information flow is totally up to the network's participants, not to companies, as in the previous stages. Two main types of social relationship networks deserve to be outlined: blogs and virtual communities.

Blogs and the Blogosphere

According to Merriam-Webster, *blog* was the most searched-for word in its online dictionary in 2004.[3] Its meaning: "online shared diary, where people add entries about their personal experience and hobbies." A blog is an Internet page that allows its author (or authors) to easily publish information and calls for "posts" or articles, which are available according to the order in which they are published. The blog has a calendar and an area for readers' comments.

Why should blogs, or simply online diaries, be an area of attention for companies? According to Technorati,[4] 120,000 new blogs are created daily, there are 70 million blogs all over the world, and 1.5 million posts are created every day by the participants in these blogs. These figures are impressive enough to attract the attention of companies that want to expose their brands and their products.

However, in order to understand how to reach these people, companies must concentrate on the blogosphere and not the blogs themselves.

The blogosphere is the collective term used to represent the universe of all blogs within the virtual community. According to Wikipedia,[5] "Blogs are only examples of a certain choice of format, while the blogosphere is a social phenomenon. What differentiates blogs from other internet pages is that the first are part of a social network formed by two-handed links among different blogs. You make a link to my articles, I make a link for yours and both will be more interesting."

Through the links created in the blogs, it is possible to determine the interconnection between them. The more links a blog receives and points out, the greater its area of influence in the virtual community and its density in the net. Credibility, in this case, is measured by the blog's relevance, not just the coverage of its traffic. When we analyze the distribution of blogs with regard to their influence, we can observe three different levels of links:

- There are a thousand blogs that exhibit from 1,000 to more than 60,000 different links.
- There are 155,000 blogs that exhibit from 20 to 1,000 links.
- The millions of remaining blogs exhibit 20 links at most.

When an article published in a blog catches the interest of the community, it goes to all other blogs through the links built among them. The time required for the information to reach all other blogs depends on the number of connections it has to make. In general, the information moves faster when it departs from a high-density network blog. Many times, a subject of high interest can go through a great part of the blogosphere and reach millions of people in only a few hours.

Virtual Communities and Discussion Forums

Before the launch of the World Wide Web and the commercial use of the Internet, people already used computer networks to exchange information and resolve doubts in several areas.

Starting in 1980, the so-called USENET network was created to facilitate exchanges among students, teachers, and researchers at American universities. Participants created discussion groups about different topics and sent and received messages by e-mail.

Although the first groups focused on technical subjects, the topics soon began to include other matters, such as music, sports, and drugs. Through CompuServe, the discussion forums that existed in the academic universe began to be used in the commercial field.

In 1990, America Online established itself as the biggest provider of this type of service, giving popularity to several communities, such as Motley Fool for individual investors, Blackberry Creek for teenagers, and Senior Net for the adult population.

The discussion forums of the past progressed in more sophisticated dynamic systems, known as virtual communities. The creation of this term has been attributed to the book with the same title written by Howard Rheingold in 1993.[6] Current participants can send and receive e-mails from people in the group; exchange music, image, and video files; participate in online games; and buy through electronic commerce. Some communities, such as Friendster, offer services for the creation of individual blogs to their associates. Others, such as Second Life, innovate by their differentiated interface, where individuals can be represented through avatars, or visual representations, that are materialized through a tri-dimensional presence. In this community, all attractions, objects, and events, also in three dimensions, are created by the inhabitants themselves and belong to them.

To integrate the virtual communities, their members fill out information regarding their profiles—for instance, their name, address, age, job, hobbies, and favorite movies. Once people are registered in such a group, they can look for other individuals with similar characteristics to get on with. In this way, they establish connections with people who otherwise would be complete strangers.

The structure of virtual communities is based on the affinity among their participants. For that to happen, it is essential that individuals in the community experience the feeling of belonging to the group and identifying themselves with it, influencing the group and also being influenced by it, and integrating the group through everybody's support. That makes them maintain an open dialogue and an enlightened community atmosphere.

Today, discussion forums and relationship communities already reach tens of millions of people. According to Wikipedia,[7] the number of people engaged in these spaces is about 265 million.

Both the blogosphere and the virtual communities present great opportunities and risks for companies because of the great number of interconnected people and the extensive number of posts that are created every day. The participants in social networks often talk about companies and products. Companies that do not manage the discussions of their brands in this field run the risk of losing sales and destroying their reputation.

Mobile marketing: the new digital connection of the crowds

The use of wireless media offers a new range of possibilities to brands. Its most compelling aspect, mobility, allows continuous interaction with consumers. This means that companies don't need to wait for individuals to access their computer or watch TV to reach them. They can have ubiquitous, always-on presence and dialogue with them.

Although we see new products with embedded wireless technology every day, the cellular phone has the most prominent position in the wireless space, surpassing the mark of 3 billion active units sold worldwide in 2007. The technology currently available transcends by far basic voice service. Data transference allows message exchange, the reading of e-mails and news, downloading of applications, and financial transactions like account checking and bill payment. With broadband resources available, it is possible to watch films, send messages with pictures captured through embedded cameras, and watch TV programming.

Mobile marketing strategies do not stand alone. They use wireless media as an integrated content delivery and direct response vehicle within a cross-channel marketing communications program. The most widely used messaging vehicle for mobile marketing is SMS (short message service). It basically consists of text messages about 160 characters long (which can be sent from one handset to another, or between a handset and a computer) and common short codes (which are phone numbers, usually four to six digits, to which the text messages can be sent). In order to participate in mobile marketing campaigns based on SMS, consumers register their mobile number, texting a keyword to a short code promoted on- or offline, through TV commercials, radio, print, web sites, digital signage, or POP displays.

In consumer acquisition campaigns, for instance, individuals are invited to send a text message to a short code in order to participate in a contest. The promotion can ask the entrants to perform an action, such as answering trivia questions or submitting an essay. The winners get a grand prize or a gift card certificate. In retention and loyalty campaigns retailers can market to their customers in order to bring them to the stores when they text special promotion sales codes. Mobile couponing enables marketers to promote loyalty strategies even further by sending a mobile coupon via text message containing the offer, the redemption code, and the coupon expiration date. The coupon can then be redeemed at the sales register in the store or at a customer service center.

The number of SMS users attests to its popularity. According to the Mobile Marketing Association,* in the U.S., 35 percent of wireless users send at least one text message a month. Worldwide, there are twice as many SMS users as there are e-mail users. Other wireless technologies like WAP and Mobile Web, Bluetooth and Mobile search, although currently less widely used, can have a similarly significant impact on mobile marketing strategies. Others will certainly surface in the near future.

However, independently of the mobile technology adopted, in order to achieve the best response rates, marketing campaigns should rely on relationship strategies to promote evolving links between the brand and consumers. This means that permission marketing premises, further explained in the next chapter, should support them. For now suffice it to say that in order to interact with any individual, marketers need to obtain consent through explicit opt-in. No direct communication should be initiated without the previous endorsement of the target base. In the same way, users must be able to exercise their opt-out choice, terminating the process to receive messages at will. When marketers support consumer privacy standards and use database support to gather consumer data during mobile marketing campaigns, they ensure the best use of one of the most pervasive channels available nowadays.

The big opportunity
Every year, millions of people around the globe become Internet surfers by simply connecting their PCs to the World Wide Web. However, this can be more strongly observed in developed countries, where, due to a more horizontal income distribution, the dominant middle classes can more easily purchase a computer and pay for Internet services.

---

* www.mmaglobal.com

Taking a global look at the Internet, the same does not happen in developing countries, where only a minority of the population can afford a computer and an Internet connection. Activities such as online media, commerce, culture, and communication are restricted to a minority.

With mobile technology, on the other hand, especially cellular phone technology, an important portion of the population in the lower economic classes can have access to the online network. This becomes apparent when we analyze the list of the largest cellular markets globally. Of the top five positions, four belong to the emergent BRIC countries, Brazil, Russia, India and China. Exploring the penetration of mobile technology into different segments of the society, marketers have an important opportunity to develop one-to-one relationship marketing strategies on a massive scale.

Key Points

- Relationship marketing can play a key role in the integration of a brand's communications. We know that companies enjoy a range of options for points of contact with their target public, such as communication vehicles, fairs and promotional events, the Internet, points of sale, and customer service centers. Being present at several points of contact requires the several types of communication involved to adopt a consistent message when it comes to brand positioning. The communication is plural, but the message must be unique and personalized.
- In multidisciplinary campaigns, it is desirable to have horizontal harmony among the different media—unified concepts, texts, and images—so that each reinforces the others, providing the consumer with a unique perception of the brand. Vertical harmony is also necessary, caring for the

sequential use of various communication channels that complement one another in order to maintain the brand's constant presence in the mind of the consumer. Therefore, integrated communication is based on the strategic orchestration of existing media. In general, it requires the support of several vendors, such as agencies that handle marketing, advertising, public relations, promotion, and the Web. If you position the individual consumer at the center of all marketing decisions, you will ensure that the various participants work toward the same goals. The main objective is to fully develop each person's relationship curve with the brand. As a result, it is necessary to segment the target public based on already identified marketing objectives and employ the most appropriate channels for each group in a complementary manner.

- Internet and direct marketing already explore individualized communications to maximize results. Advertising, promotion, events, and public relations, in turn, are based on mass communication, in which uniform treatment of the customer base is assured. However, these disciplines also can be folded into integrated communication programs. They just need to be planned and coordinated from a relationship marketing perspective, rather than as independent communication solutions.

CHAPTER 5

Creating Results

The fact that the creative component plays a major role in determining the results of communication activities is undeniable. A well-defined creation leads to exactly the desired response. When the public is receptive to a message and responds satisfactorily, that is an infallible path to achieving the marketing professional's objectives.

The main challenge is to identify a strong marketing concept and its intellectual and emotional components, which together create successful campaigns. Throughout this chapter, we will analyze the factors involved and describe the necessary steps in developing a creative plan that will have a positive impact on relationship-marketing programs.

Creating Attitude or Generating Behavior

When conceptualizing the essence of the development of a creative plan, it is possible to understand the different and complementary characteristics of mass media and direct-response advertisements by analyzing consumers' varying reactions to these two types of communication. It also becomes clear that the routes to results with these two types of approaches are diametrically opposed.

Mass media advertising influences the consumer's attitude. It establishes a path with recall and awareness of the brand and then generates enough goodwill so that the purchase occurs. The creation of direct-response advertisements, in contrast, aims to stimulate new behavior in the consumer, leading to a quick and direct response (call to action). Thus, direct-response advertising must be broader and more detailed in its description of product benefits and price. Furthermore, it is of the utmost importance to provide the consumer with the response channels and available payment systems as part of the creative process. Thus, in order to be irresistible and inspire the consumer to spend, it must be "tailor-made for the consumer," satisfying personal yearnings and expectations. The inherent reasoning for each of these two types of communication determines how the plan's creation is elaborated in each of the cases. According to Godin,[1] mass marketing is based on interruption marketing, whereas direct-response advertising is sustained by the concept of permission marketing.

Interruption Marketing

For years, mass-marketing professionals have used interruption marketing to grab the attention of the target public. The television commercial, carefully inserted into the programming schedule, interrupts viewers while they are enjoying a TV show. Ads in magazines and newspapers, which are placed in between articles, interrupt readers. Billboards on city streets interrupt drivers and pedestrians as they move to and from their homes and workplaces. In all of these examples, the procedure is the same: interrupt people who are engaged in activities and grab their attention to show a message from the company. The hope is that the communication will arouse the interest of a certain portion of the viewers.

However, as the number of interruptions increases, their effectiveness decreases. Competing for the same valuable commodity—people's time—companies clamor to fill communication vehicles with messages. In top-rated programs, it is not uncommon for all television commercials to last almost the same time of the entire program! There are magazines in which for every page of news, there is another full page of advertising. According to Stone and Jacobs,[2] the ratio of advertising to content in consumer magazines is around 50–50. In the case of local television programming, the proportion is around 60 percent for programming and 40 percent for advertising. In some cities, there are areas where billboards cover entire buildings, completely changing the landscape. And the population's response can be swift and sure. If the visual pollution of billboards reaches unbearable limits, neighborhood associations launch campaigns to demand their removal. If the TV commercial is too long, audiences start channel surfing, searching for a better option. If print publications are chock full of ads, readers look for something else to read. The positive results expected from the interruption decline dramatically as the number of interruptions increases.

The proliferation of new channels further aggravates the situation. There are hundreds of television channels, radio stations, and magazines available. Digital TV will permit the viewer to select from among approximately 500 different channels. If a person takes 5 seconds, on average, to check out another program, the total time needed to see all of the options exceeds 40 minutes! Where can you find your desired public? How can you make your message stand out in the midst of such clutter? How can you catch the audience's attention for even a short period of time?

One recourse is to explore the range of locations where people can be found. Nowadays, we find messages on buses, on taxis, in commercial building elevators, and even on city garbage containers! Another option is to create stimulating communications with distinct formats. Multimedia billboards have used video resources, three-dimensional objects, and even human beings as live sculptures. Recently in Japan, vertical games were created on a billboard to highlight Adidas's sport products. Two players, attached to a billboard on the top of a 10-story building, played soccer, moving back and forth while held by special ropes. They kicked a ball that hung from a rope between them.

However, the most effective way to shine a light on your message in the midst of so many is to repeat the communication frequently. The more often a message interrupts the audience, the better the chances that it will be noticed. A television commercial stays on the air for several weeks. A print ad in a magazine runs in several editions. The impact on the consumer base is similar to that of osmosis: the message will gradually seep in until it is completely absorbed.

The biggest obstacle to this strategy is escalating costs. Generally, running the same ads twice doubles the price. For most companies, airing or publishing an ad in the mass media over and over again is financially prohibitive. The only companies that are able to stand out amidst the clutter of ads are those that have a large enough marketing budget to repeat their messages as many times as necessary to get the attention of their target public. In some cases, the cheapest alternative is to use a small number of repetitions and disperse the message among several different vehicles in the hope that a larger number of people will be reached. This is one of the biggest mistakes made by marketing professionals who do not understand the inner dynamics of interruption marketing. Communication coverage—the number of individuals exposed to a communication at least once during a specific period of time—is not the most important factor. The number of repetitions of the message to which individuals are exposed is the determining variable that highlights that particular message among so many others.

Another relevant issue is the balance between communication coverage and message richness. According to Evans and Wurster,[3] the more people the contact channel is able to reach, the less complex the sent message will be. For example, an electronic vehicle has the capacity to reach most homes. On the other hand, the space available for this type of commercial is often no more than a few seconds. Each ad in a magazine or newspaper with national circulation occupies a small printed space. However, as we migrate to channels that have less coverage, communication richness increases. It is not uncommon for communications to last several minutes in active telemarketing, in which thousands of people are reached. The space available to explore communication with the target public in this case is much broader than with the electronic channel, but, on the other hand, the infrastructure required and the costs involved are prohibitive if you intend to reach millions of people. At the other end of the spectrum, there are individualized pitches from the sales force, an option that is present in different circumstances in the business market. Message richness is maximized, as are the limitations on its ability to reach a large audience.

The dynamic of mass communication is based on interrupting people. It requires high frequency in order to stand out from the competition. There is extensive coverage of the base, but message richness is limited. There is little space for detailed descriptions of the company or its products and services. There is no opening for interaction with the target public; communication is unidirectional, from the brand to the market.

Analyzed from the consumers' perspective, interruption marketing is intrusive. It interrupts the movie they are watching; the same commercial they have no interest in seeing is repeated over and over; it visually pollutes the city with billboards spread over buildings, parks, and avenues; and it crams the newspapers with more ads than news. Isn't there any other way for companies to communicate their offerings?

Permission Marketing

The alternative to interruption marketing is called *permission marketing*. Consumer rejection of the massive amount of unsolicited communication can be used as a competitive advantage. With this alternative, companies must ask for permission from the individuals before sending the message. When authorized, they create a dialogue channel with the base where interaction is permitted, and therefore, dispersion (i.e., the number of people reached who never will acquire the products) is eliminated. Thus, the need for high amounts of investment to catch people's attention is replaced by the allocation of resources for strategies that continuously develop the relationship with the target public.

The first natural consequence of this strategy is that a dialogue is established between the sender and the receiver of the message. The objective of every created communication is to arouse the interest of individuals, stimulating some call to action. This mechanism has a significant impact on the entire creative process. It is not enough to develop communication programs that act only within the sphere of brand perception. It is also necessary to address the behavior component. Thus, creative pieces need to have prominent areas that direct individuals toward response channels where they can register their identities and buy. The inclusion in an ad of an Internet address or a phone number for contact establishes a means whereby people can seek more information about the content being presented, eliminate doubts, formalize complaints, and even request more personalized contact from companies that operate in the business market. Here, the creative challenge is to develop actions that simultaneously stimulate consumer response *and* increase brand perception.

In order for individuals to authorize dialogue with a company, its messages must follow three basic principles. First, the communication needs to be expected and requested. In other words, the sending of the messages must be authorized. Unsolicited communication is intrusive and misconstrues the main objective of permission marketing, which is to develop and strengthen the company's relationship with its customer base. Rather than being a cheap way to reach your target public, the various e-mails that cram inboxes with unsolicited ads create an inverse reaction, causing Internet users to lose interest in checking them.

Individuals should formally grant permission for the company to send promotional communications before any messages are sent to them. Permission can be requested and secured when users are visiting the corporate site, registering their purchase of products, or calling consumer support services, or at any other available moment. What is fundamental is for people to select the topics and situations for which they wish to be contacted.

The company must show that it will respect the choices that individuals make and always have a mechanism available allowing people to cancel the previous option. The decision to begin or interrupt the dialogue is the consumer's prerogative, and he or she should control the dynamics of the relationship with the brand. The company's role is to feed and stimulate this dialogue.

The second principle of permission marketing is that it's personal in nature. The individuals who authorize the dialogue expect the communication to be personalized, directed at them. They are not interested in standard messages that do not satisfy their expectations. The mass treatment found in interruption marketing must be replaced with an individualized message that promotes the perception of a one-to-one relationship. This can be achieved by using a simple technique such as inserting the addressee's name in the body of the communication, or through more refined solutions that personalize the content according to each person's profile.

Technological advances in recent years have made it possible to develop sophisticated solutions for applying customized mass marketing. By combining collaborative filter techniques, data mining, and business rules, new systems permit the personalization of individualized communication based on each person's behavior history. The Internet user who visits Amazon's site in search of a book receives a series of publication suggestions related to the previous purchase. Based on the current selection, the site shows other books purchased by people with the same interests. Authorized promotional e-mails are periodically sent announcing new releases by the person's favorite author. The one-click resource that is available on the site eliminates the need to fill out credit card and mailing address information every time a new purchase is made. By recovering previously registered data, personalization facilitates the commercial transaction and makes the dialogue more convenient.

In some cases, personalization can be completely automated. In others, it demands human intervention, such as thinking up answers to specific consumer questions. In any of the alternatives, permission marketing's most important aim is to have people perceive the relationship as unique and believe that the company wants to understand their individual needs so that it can satisfy them.

The final principle behind permission marketing is that communication is relevant. Without this, the message will not arouse the desired interest. Personalization will be of little worth, and the previously selected authorization will be canceled. For this not to happen, the company must constantly update its database with the subjects of greatest relevance to its base. Forms can be used to identify the most looked-for topics. When a new customer subscribes to a newspaper and agrees to receive complementary content by e-mail, the selection of subjects of interest is a unique opportunity for the company to personalize the online content in a relevant manner. In addition to the appropriate selection of content, the information must be updated. It is useless to send e-mail news every week of sports results that happened several days ago.

The interested party has probably already found the information from other sources.

Once again, the consumer conducts the dialogue with the brand. He or she identifies what is relevant, and the company seeks to provide it. When the search for a specific subject ceases, related messages also should cease. When new categories of interest arise, new content ought to be formatted.

With permission marketing, the consumer controls the dialogue, authorizing the communication that he or she wishes to receive over the most convenient channels and in the desired time frame. In this environment, factors like frequency, coverage, and the richness of the message operate differently from the way they operate in interruption marketing, implying the need for different methods of creative developments, as we will see later.

When communication is authorized and the number of messages increases, it is because the consumer is satisfied and demands a more continuous and intense dialogue with the brand. Therefore, it is not an interruption instrument, but a tool to increase both the dialogue and the relationship. The same television commercial can be repeated several times. On the other hand, when the same e-mail message is delivered over and over again, people immediately complain. It is not expected that this channel will be used in an intrusive manner. Therefore, in a dialogue, it is unacceptable for one of the parties to insist on repeating the same message.

The idea of coverage is replaced by the concept of segmentation. It is more important to direct investments to the segment of the public that accounts for the biggest chunk of company profits, rather than applying resources uniformly to the entire base. The company should allocate more resources to those customers who offer greater value.

In this case, the vividness and power of the message are in direct proportion to the importance of the segment. The three-dimensional direct-mail pieces that require more resources are sent to more profitable customers. Letters and postcards with lower costs are directed to the consumers who are of moderate importance. E-mail marketing pieces complete the program, and they are sent to the rest of the base. Digital messages travel over the Internet at practically no cost. The emergence of technical standards for communication, such as the IP, TCP, HTTP, HTML, and XML protocols, along with the great connection capacity of electronic networks, shifts the balance between coverage and message richness in an online context. On the Internet, communications can be quite complex, and at the same time, coverage may reach the total number of users online. The technical and financial obstacles to sending the message disappear. So the challenge for the professional is to identify the size that is big enough to create impact, but not so big that it results in information overload for the consumer.

From a creative point of view, permission-marketing principles establish guidelines that are diametrically opposed to those found in interruption marketing. First, communication must be personalized. Second, frequency is defined by the user, and the richness of the message is directly proportional to the importance of the targeted segment.

But how can we find the optimal level of personalization? How do we determine the appropriate length for a message? What are relationship marketing's procedures for identifying the application of creative elements that define how to build the best communication pieces according to the principles just outlined? The answers to these questions are testing, testing, and testing.

The Consumer Defines the Creation

Two different creative focuses are tested in pilot campaigns, with the objective of identifying which of them will have the greater return. Could a highlighted illustration in an e-mail piece help increase response rates? By developing one piece with the illustration and another without it, and then randomly sending each creation to a different sample of the selected base, the marketing professional is able to test which solution is preferred. To guarantee a higher rate of return, does direct-mail content need to be brief or long? Once again, the creation of two pieces, one short and one long, will help gauge the best approach.

The important thing is to notice that formal measurement adds a new dimension to marketing strategies. First of all, speculation concerning the public's intentions and behaviors is replaced by proven and measured actions. The famous "guessometer" cedes its seat to the observation of facts. After that, the program's creative component is directed toward obtaining results, not toward creative excesses. The latter have often become the final goal and, as a result, have interfered with reading communications accurately. In contrast, testing and creation do not compete with each other. In fact, they work together to maximize consumer response.

Creative professionals have gained experience in the techniques necessary for applying response tests. In some situations, they are able to predict which actions will achieve the best results even before the tests are developed. In others, accumulated knowledge is not sufficient to guarantee the best choice of action. When this happens, the best alternative is to develop a battery of tests for a sample of targeted users, and from the results obtained, duplicate the best option for the rest of the base. Rather than compare only two options at a time, it is also possible to try the tactic of testing several factors simultaneously. In these cases, it is not uncommon for the winning option to obtain two or three times as many responses as the other alternatives.[4]

Working the Creation Variables

Which factors should be tested? What are the available alternatives? Different aspects of the medium can interfere with the existing options, depending on the communication channel being used. For example, the test for the best animation time for introducing a product in an e-mail marketing piece will rarely have a parallel in a direct-mail message. In another case, tactile sensory variables, such as type of paper and the three-dimensionality that are inherent in direct mail, are not available for analysis in a digital or electronic ad.

The following is a list of questions, answers, and comments detailing the primary factors that can hinder effective direct communication campaigns. The marketing professional should use this list to develop a battery of response tests so as to determine the best creative combination for communication efforts.

Print Media: Testing Magazines and Newspapers

1. Should insert cards be used? These are creative pieces that are inserted in publications and contain product information. In general, they cost more than ads.
2. Should reply cards be used? These cards allow the reader to request information or make a purchase. They are postage paid, thus eliminating mailing costs for the interested party.
3. Is there a time of year when response rates tend to be higher? The effect of seasons must be taken into account.
4. Frequency: what is the optimal number of insertions per period? The response to each insertion is worth more than a response to an ad.
5. What is the ideal size for an ad? The larger the space, the greater the visibility. However, does the additional cost result in greater returns? Almost never.
6. Should the ad be black and white, two colors, or four colors? In some vehicles, costs vary according to the choice. Will the use of more colors increase the response rate?
7. Does the location of an ad in a magazine make a difference in terms of reader response? Experience shows that ads give higher

returns the closer they are to the first page. Ads on pages on the right, or on odd-numbered pages, also provide better response rates than ads on even-numbered pages. Here are some response rates of pages based on their proximity to the first page, which for comparison purposes is rated 100 percent:

- First page: 100 percent
- Second page to the right: 95 percent
- Third page to the right: 90 percent
- Fourth page to the right: 85 percent

Newspaper readers behave differently from magazine readers, especially when it comes to their response time. The newspaper is typically read the day it is delivered, or it is not read at all. For monthly magazines, the percentage of people who will eventually respond follows this model:

- After the first week: 3 percent to 7 percent
- After the second week: 20 percent to 25 percent
- After the third week: 40 percent to 45 percent
- After the first month: 50 percent to 55 percent
- After the second month: 75 percent to 85 percent
- After the third month: 85 percent to 92 percent
- After four months: 92 percent to 95 percent

The use of color in newspaper ads never reaches the quality used in magazines. However, studies show that the use of two colors in newspaper ads results in a response increase of 58 percent when compared to the use of black and white. When using four colors, this increase could reach 78 percent.

Electronic Media: Testing Network and Cable TV

In the advertising industry, the ads on TV are considered commercials, whereas response films are known as infomercials because of the extensive descriptions of product benefits, price, and other details.

1. Length of advertisements: on television, 30 seconds is the most common length for a commercial. This is hardly enough time to introduce products with all their details. Building the brand with call-to-action appeals can require more time, between 60 and 90 seconds, or even 15, 30, or 60 minutes as in the classic American infomercials.
2. Is there a broadcast time when response rates to call-to-action campaigns are higher? The time periods that provide the best returns are those when the viewers are more relaxed and primed to respond, such as later at night.
3. What is the call-to-action dimension? Should you use the 1-800 response channel or the Internet? Or both? To get the best response, flash the response channels at the top or bottom of the screen from the beginning to the end of the infomercial so that the consumer has the maximum amount of time to memorize or take note of the contact information.
4. Frequency: what is the optimal number of insertions per period? This will depend on the number of responses per insertion.

Testing Direct Mail

1. There are several options to choose from: the postcard, the self-mailer, and the classic direct-mail piece with envelope, letter, brochure, and response card.
2. In the case of the classic direct-mail piece, it is possible to use extra windows in the envelope to highlight topics of greater importance. The envelope can be semitransparent or use special paper, so long as the weight of the entire mailing keeps the postal fee level to that which is most appropriate for the action's budget.
3. Should the letter be short or long? How many lines should each paragraph have? In general, paragraphs should have a maximum of six to seven lines. The most important ideas should be highlighted. More than one color can be used to reinforce these points.

4. There should be several different versions of the same letter, each aimed at a different segment of the consumer base. Customizing letters will make the approach more effective

5. The letters should be personalized. Use the consumer's name and a personal tone. The text should show that you are always ready to serve him or her well and in a timely manner.

6. The response card should be simple, direct, easy to read, and interactive, suggesting reader involvement.

7. The return rate is higher when a gift is offered. In some cases, these gifts can cause an increase in the response rate of up to 25 percent. What type of gift should be given? Experience shows that perceived value is the most important thing. Therefore, let your creativity roam and seek pertinence.

8. The pieces can contain icons highlighting topics of interest.

Testing the Internet: Banners, E-mails, and Sites

Banners

1. Banner formats: HTML or rich media? In the latter case, it is imperative for the target public to have high-speed Internet connections. Otherwise, the impact of the communication will be very frustrating for the Internet user.

2. The text should include a strong call to action, attracting responses.

3. Banner colors should stand out on the page.

4. How often should banners be updated? According to Doubleclick, a U.S. online advertising firm, Internet users are more likely to click on banners the first time they see them. The response curve to banner ads has a sharp slope, indicating that it is possible to measure effectiveness a few hours after the ads are shown.

5. The banner should have a simple message and should not be loaded with images, text, and animation.

6. The banner can be interactive and permit the user to select some option before being directed to another page on the Internet.

7. Does the banner have a better response rate than the pop-up or other media format? Always test the alternatives to find the best results.

E-mail

1. Is an Internet user opt-in required for sending an e-mail? Yes. Otherwise, it is characterized as spam, or unsolicited e-mail, which goes against the principles of permission marketing.
2. What is the company's response time for an e-mail question raised by a consumer? Immediate. Excessive delay significantly compromises the Internet user's expectations, reducing the chances of success for future actions.
3. The e-mail should provide the option for the user to unsubscribe.
4. The e-mail piece should not be full of texts and images.
5. The privacy policy for using subscriber information should be clear and transparent.
6. The security policy spelling out the impossibility of the company's e-mail message containing a virus should be highlighted.
7. Test the best time for the user to receive an e-mail.
8. Do not abuse access by sending frequent e-mails to the same target public.
9. The best e-mails are personalized.
10. Choose the e-mail subject heading well to attract the most interest.
11. Which e-mail formats should be tested? Only text, text with static images, or text with animated images.
12. Use call-to-action resources extensively.
13. The e-mail should inspire the consumer to interact.

Sites

1. Call-to-action language should always be used.
2. Do the registration forms have fields that are pertinent to the stage of the relationship with the visitor? Internet users are turned off by long forms.

3. The utilization policy involving gathered data must be clear and transparent.
4. Ideally, the site should be personalized to recognize the Internet user whenever he or she returns, customizing the information according to his or her interests. Find out the degree of customization that should be reached in each case.
5. There can be several levels of navigation on the site. But do not pile on the average number of pages that the user must go through to get to the information of interest.
6. How does it look and feel to explore the site? Creativity is a good thing, but make sure to use clear text, images, and animations.
7. How does the site become more attractive when interactive resources are used? There are simulators, games, chat rooms, and other good resources.

Years of experience have taught direct-marketing professionals that identifying practical rules for developing effective communications is of the utmost importance. In some cases, these guidelines can be applied to a broad range of companies. In others, they may be more appropriate for specific industries. However, the greatest reward is having developed a strong set of guidelines that enable every marketing professional to systematically test his or her campaigns on the target public.

The list of options for each channel shared in this chapter isn't intended to reveal every possible alternative but is merely a basic reference tool. It was based on work by the Rapp Collins group, which has years of experience in creating global relationship-marketing campaigns, as well on literature by great experts in the field of direct communication, such as Stone, who has already been mentioned. As marketing professionals test the communication pieces and learn which obtain the best results, they add the variables that have the greatest impact on the action's return rates to the list. The best way to understand how each variable behaves is by developing pilot campaigns that test the various alternatives.

Test Models

There are two kinds of large, practical experiments that can be used to develop relationship-marketing tests—either test one parameter at a time or test a combination of them. In the first case, the desired parameter is chosen. Each of the possible variations is shown to different groups of customers. Assuming that all other components are constant, the alternative with the greatest response provides the optimal value for the analyzed variable. For example, to identify the importance of the gift in a demand generation action using direct mail, four different alternatives can be studied:

- Piece 1: no gift
- Piece 2: with a gift worth $50.00
- Piece 3: with a gift worth $100.00
- Piece 4: with a gift worth $200.00

Four random samples should be chosen from the base, one for each pilot action. If the other creative components are the same for all four pieces—specifically, the envelope, letter, brochure, and response card—then in each case, the amount of demand generated will identify the relative importance of the gift. If the number of responses is substantially higher with Piece 4 and the increase is sufficient to cover the higher cost, then a more significant investment in gifts should be made and the rest of the base should be offered gifts. At the other extreme, if the responses are similar for all four segments, clearly Piece 1 should be chosen.

Testing one factor at a time can require many experiments because of the great number of alternatives for existing variables. This extensive testing can greatly increase costs. Another limitation of this procedure is that it may ignore effects resulting from a combination of factors. For example, in the previous case, if Piece 1, without a gift, is combined with a letter containing a strong call to action, it could achieve returns similar to those achieved by the other alternatives.

Another form of experiment is one that tests a combination of factors all at once. In this case, the marketing professional should choose the combinations, typically based on the results from past experiences. Of course, many alternatives will be disregarded as a result of prejudgment, and some could have great impact. On the other hand, when a combination stands out from the rest, it is difficult to know exactly which parameters were responsible for the action's success.

Statistical test models based on experimental designs can eliminate the limitation of procedures by adding a scientific discipline. They require personnel who specialize in such test methods and who can increase the complexity in administering pilot campaigns. In some cases, the returns achieved are sufficient to compensate the company for the investments made. For more details about these methods, consult Shepard.[5]

In relationship marketing, the philosophy behind the communication is based on permission-marketing principles in that a dialogue is established with consumers as a way to break through the deluge of messages that they receive via multiple channels. This two-way street is the foundation upon which the relationship grows. The creation of the communication feeds this dynamic. It results in interactivity, involving the target public with messages that stimulate and promote responses with call-to-action techniques.

Using creative parameters in pilot campaigns increases the return rates further, improving the brand's relationship with its public. In this new stage, when the consumer has control of the action, the creation of attractive communication pieces is no longer sufficient. The pieces must promote dialogue. Otherwise, they will serve only as a means for getting awards for creativity at industry contests.

Key Points

- Creation plays a fundamental role in what communication campaigns ultimately accomplish. But the way to achieve results in mass media communication and direct-response communication differs significantly. Whereas mass media communication works to affect consumer behavior by creating a brand identity and convincing the consumer to make the purchase at the point of sale someday, direct-response communication aims to inspire new behavior, a faster and more direct consumer response. As a result, the latter needs to be more persuasive and more detailed in its description of product benefits and qualities. The intrinsic logic of each type of communication establishes the way creation is developed.

- Mass media communication is based on interruption marketing; TV commercials, for instance, interrupt a movie or program to catch the attention of the target public. However, as the number of interruptions increases, the effectiveness of this strategy decreases. Communication is unidirectional, from the brand to the market, and it needs high frequency to get noticed amid all the competition.

- An alternative to interruption marketing is called permission marketing. Here, companies ask for permission from the individuals before sending the message and create a dialogue and channel for interaction with the base. In order for dialogue to be possible, the messages must satisfy three basic principles: they must be authorized, personalized, and relevant. Here, the objective of the communication is to arouse the interest of individuals, stimulating some call to action. The consumer controls the dialogue, authorizing the communication that he or she wishes to receive over the most convenient channels and in the desired time frame.

From a creative point of view, pilot campaigns are used to test the different channels and variables with the objective of identifying the option that provides the greatest return. The program's creative component is directed toward obtaining results, not toward the creativity excesses that often become the final objective, thus interfering with the reading of the communication.

CHAPTER 6

Relationship Marketing in Action

In the previous chapters, we discussed how relationship marketing reorganizes the communication functions so as to focus on establishing a personalized connection with consumers, in every stage of the individual's relationship with the brand, from awareness to the postsale phase. The payoff can be a high rate of return on investment. The question that arises for the marketing professional is: how can a relationship-marketing program be put into action? In this chapter, we will explore the practical aspects of implementing such a program in greater detail, including all the necessary steps for launching a communication campaign.

The first step is to plan the program in stages so as to guarantee the delivery of each part. But before that program can be developed, you need to conduct an in-depth analysis of the target public, the available communication channels, and the goals of the communication campaign. And you need to make sure that the goals are in sync with the company's general marketing strategy. That will help you progress smoothly into the subsequent stages of creation and control.

Rapp Collins developed a technique called Insight CRM that uses the specifications of the different stages to develop relationship programs. The primary objective is to ensure that the marketing professional creates and implements the actions consistently, from the specification of objectives to the analysis of results. This process has four phases: strategic analysis, planning, implementation, and control. Each will be explained in detail in the following pages.

Phase 1: Strategic Analysis

In relationship marketing, it is always necessary to begin with the most comprehensive perspective possible. Marketing professionals are often so anxious to implement the campaign that they act without adequate deliberation. Before they've even laid out the program's strategy, they've begun to develop the communication pieces. That is a mistake. The first step is to analyze the fundamentals necessary for the implementation phases and clearly identify the main objective of the marketing campaign.

Four basic questions must be answered:

1. What are the customer segments you're targeting, specifically their behavioral and transactional profiles with regard to the brand?
2. What type of offer will have high perceived value, and in which channels and when should it be presented?
3. What is the expected financial return on the investment?
4. What is the infrastructure required to support and execute the program?

Each of these questions will be analyzed here.

The First Question: What Is the Target Public's Profile?

Which group of individuals do you wish to reach in each campaign? Part of this answer is directly linked to the marketing objectives of the action. As discussed in Chapter 3, the stages of the relationship can be identified as awareness, consideration, conversion, and postsale. First, it is necessary to map the entire existing base to see which phase each individual is in at that moment, as selecting the target public for a campaign requires choosing a group of people who are in the same relationship stage with the brand. To guarantee that the message is precise, complementary segmentation of these groups is required based on their demographic, behavioral, or transactional attributes (for more information on such segmentation, see Chapter 7). Identifying the exact value of each audience member will help you determine how much should be invested to reap a certain projected return.

Generally, to get a complete picture of the target public, you must identify the complete set of variables that characterize the base. This first step has the objective of taking each member's relationship stage with the brand into account when selecting the marketing program to be applied. During the awareness, consideration, and conversion stages, winning strategies based on PRM or member-get-member programs should be applied. For those customers who are in the postsale stage, use maintenance strategies based on loyalty and retention campaigns. As for those who abandoned the brand, develop recovery programs with the mission of reintegrating the former customers.

During the message formulation stage, it is helpful to determine the individual consumer needs based on their profiles. For example, financial products that are cross-sold are directly related to the age of the target public. Sales promotions of pension products tend to get the best responses from middle-aged individuals, whereas life insurance products appeal predominantly to older age groups. Gender, income bracket, and the frequency and value of previous purchases can also be incorporated into detailed descriptions of the base, making the picture even more precise. To make sure that you focus on the most salient factors, it is essential that you identify the correlation coefficient between the selected attributes and the projected rate of response for the campaigns.

Finally, the "value" variable inserts the financial dimension into the description of the base. Since investment resources are scarce, allocation must follow the logic of maximum return on invested capital. This means that top priority should be given to implementing campaigns targeting those segments with the most valuable customers. In those cases, communication resources tend to offer more options with implementation time more reduced.

The Second Question: What Is the Offer, and In Which Channels and Moments It Should Be Available?

Once the target public has been identified, the next step is to define the marketing actions to be taken for each segment and also define the most appropriate channels to use. Each group's relationship stage helps determine the program schedule for activities aimed at that group. For example, in campaigns to acquire new customers, retail chains can use merchandise clearance programs, special promotions, and celebrations on store inauguration for the public. For loyalty campaigns, celebration dates that mark holidays such as Mother's Day, Valentine's Day, Christmas, and New Year's Day can be explored.

Select the best channel for each of the actions (see Figure 6.1). A sale offer for a new product can be communicated through a direct-mail piece, while a birthday greeting can be sent by e-mail. An invitation to participate in a certain event can use the active telemarketing channel, while a trial of the product takes place at the point of sale. Channel alternatives should be explored, with the objective of providing the most convenient means for individuals to interact with the brand. Map out all contact possibilities and select those that offer the greatest likelihood of response relative to the necessary investments. There are customers who prefer the Internet because of its speed and ease of personalization. Others are more accustomed to receiving print catalogs and skimming through the pages of offers. Many customers consider a visit to a point of sale a form of leisure and fun. For example,

Figure 6.1   Best Channel for Each Action

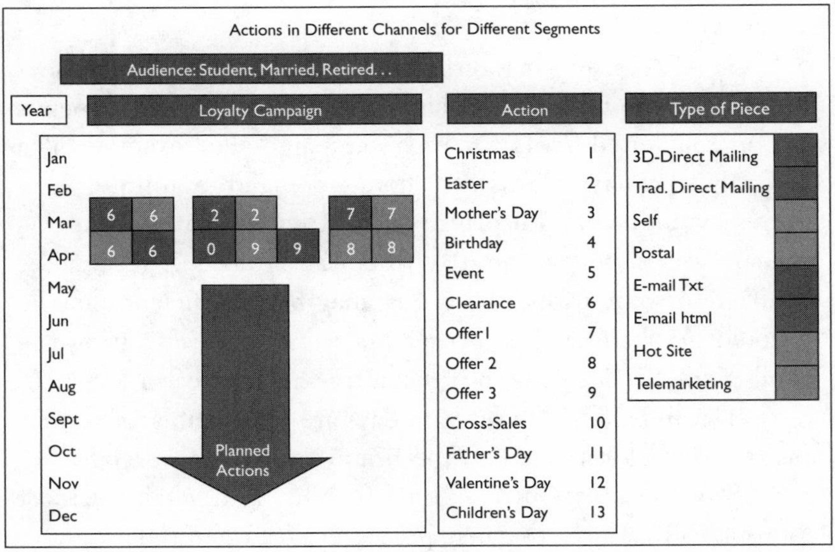

Actions in Different Channels for Different Segments

Audience: Student, Married, Retired...

Year	Loyalty Campaign	Action		Type of Piece
Jan		Christmas	1	3D-Direct Mailing
Feb		Easter	2	Trad. Direct Mailing
Mar	6 6 2 2 7 7	Mother's Day	3	Self
Apr	6 6 0 9 9 8 8	Birthday	4	Postal
May		Event	5	E-mail Txt
Jun		Clearance	6	E-mail html
Jul		Offer 1	7	Hot Site
Aug		Offer 2	8	Telemarketing
Sept		Offer 3	9	
Oct	Planned Actions	Cross-Sales	10	
Nov		Father's Day	11	
Dec		Valentine's Day	12	
		Children's Day	13	

they won't give up traveling to visit their local bank in favor of the convenience of home banking. And we must remember that there are those who use all the channels, choosing one over another based on the offer and the time they have available.

The Third Question: What Is the Financial Return?

All relationship-marketing campaigns have implementation costs, which include the costs of creating and producing communication pieces, the availability of contact channels, and the allocation of hours for the professionals involved. Costs are higher in some cases than in others, but it is always necessary to have a budget to execute any type of action. Since resources are limited, the ranking of different needs must be taken into account. The big question facing the marketing professional is whether a communication action should be developed. Cost analysis, along with the projected return for the campaigns, will lay out the answer from a financial perspective.

Every relationship-marketing action must be measured. Several metrics can be used to analyze the expected return, depending on the stated goals for each campaign. For example, if a program's primary aim is to generate demand, examining how many new individuals displayed interest in the brand's products and services will help you determine the program's success (or failure). In some cases, these data may be insufficient and the selected metric must be further fine-tuned by calculating the number of individuals with little, average, and great interest. In recovery campaigns, the relevant data are the number of former customers who returned to the brand to make a purchase. In other situations, total income or profitability achieved is the most appropriate measure. To gain a precise evaluation of the program, it is critical to use metrics that permit a comparison with established benchmarks from other campaigns. The final objective is always to create better campaigns that generate better results.

Whatever the parameters used, the feasibility analysis should be directly tied to the cost-benefit ratio. From a financial point of view, a communication campaign should be implemented if, and only if, the analysis using the selected metrics shows that it will produce a positive increase in value for the company within a determined period of time.

The Fourth Question: What Infrastructure Is Required?

The complexity of implementing relationship-marketing actions demands the use of continuous and systemic processes that produce solutions that satisfy the needs of the final consumers within the defined time frames and budgets. Identifying failures in functioning late in the process is often symptomatic of bigger problems related to undetected inconsistencies in the definition phases

of the infrastructure. The infrastructure has four main components: a database, a relationship-management tool, fulfillment
(the order, packaging, and delivery process), and response channels.
We will now explain each the roles of each of these components, as
well as the main issues involved to ensure the program's success.

Database

Great technological sophistication is needed to identify the most
relevant prospects and customers and create integrated communications in every contact channel. The company must have the ability to share the information and have high-capacity processing
systems. In general, it is possible for data on the target public to be
found in several different databases within the company. It is not
unusual for an individual to be registered in the company's transactional database with purchase information, in the customer service database with the support history, and in the Internet database
when identification forms were filled out. Data integration is a basic
condition for developing marketing communication programs.
Information records in all of the systems need to be consistent. On
the one hand, this requires the standardization of data, and on the
other, it requires the use of connectors that automatically update
the content in every legacy database when there is any activity or
amendment of an individual's attributes.

In order to provide support for relationship-marketing programs,
the databases must be able to guarantee the accurate reading of
information on the target public and to store the campaign history.
They must record the result of each communication action taken
and the individual response from each member of the audience.

Relationship-Management Tool

Managing every communication action for the different segments
of the base in the different channels manually can be painstak-
ing work. Relationship marketing uses software called relationship-management tool (RM Tool) that enables detailed control

of the entire program. This software automates a large part of the processes involved, freeing up human resources for the most important tasks.

The process functions like this: the marketing department schedules the planned activities for the different campaigns using the tool. The system automatically sends an alert to the responsible managers, informing them that an action has been planned for a segment of the base that is their responsibility. After approval, the request for delivery of the corresponding communication pieces is sent to the fulfillment group, which coordinates the address logistics for the target public. Then, the results of each campaign are entered in the tool for subsequent analytical control.

The RM Tool stores the entire history of these actions, centralizes the development process, and adds the customers' points of view at a single control point. Its advantages are decisive in guaranteeing the structured operation of the program schedule for planned campaign actions.

Fulfillment

Producing communication pieces, mapping the target public, and allocating hours to the professionals involved in the relationship programs will have limited results if the material created for and delivered to the final consumer is not of high quality and on time. When the RM Tool relays an order to the fulfillment group, several tasks need to be performed. First, stock control must guarantee that the pieces are available in the amounts needed and in good condition. Address information needs to be updated, and all of the necessary fields need to be filled in. Material handling then stamps the addressee's information on the pieces and sends them to the transport company. When the delivery contains address errors, those pieces are returned. In such cases, the fulfillment group fills out a report in the RM Tool, noting the records that have problems. The tool immediately triggers a warning to the database maintenance group, which takes the necessary measures. These records are then deactivated until they are corrected.

The fulfillment process is generally outsourced. There are companies that control material delivery offline, with large spaces for storage and resources available for transportation. In the case of the telemarketing channel, fulfillment companies have high-capacity telephone systems for receiving and making calls. In order to use online channel services, fulfillment companies have systems to send personalized e-mails in large numbers and in a short time.

Response Channels

Dialogue with the target public is a basic condition for relationship-marketing programs, and it requires not only the triggering of communication actions, but also the capacity to respond to all questions raised by individuals. When a consumer sends an e-mail to the company expressing doubts about a certain product, or when he or she calls customer service to receive instructions on how to use recently acquired merchandise, the company must attend to that customer as quickly and as thoroughly as possible. Response channels must be built with the capacity to meet the projected demand for interaction with the base. If the channels are ill equipped, the result will be that people will be poorly served and will develop a negative image of the brand. That means that not only may they walk away from any relationship with the brand, but they also may tell others about the poor service that they received, which will result in significant losses of new consumers. On the other hand, the overequipping of channels involves unnecessary expenses that will affect return on investment (ROI).

One of the most important response channels is telemarketing. These channels are open to those who are interested in obtaining additional information, making complaints, or giving suggestions over the telephone. The toll-free (or 1-800) number emerged as consumer demand, and the volume of calls surged, making the service even more popular. Companies had to expand their teams of attendants and invest in more sophisticated phone systems, including hold mechanisms so that consumers do not get impatient while waiting to be answered.

Some companies began to realize that it was advantageous to outsource these systems, giving rise to telemarketing companies. With the creation of these specialized companies, there was a new drive in the sector thanks to significant investments in technology, training, and telephony. New computers and more appropriate software emerged, permitting the collection of data in real time.

Automated solutions are used to complement consumer support services because of the high costs involved in human services. Telephone calls are answered by systems known as automatic response units (ARUs). These systems interact with the individuals, providing prerecorded responses to the most frequently asked questions. When a response is not available, an operator assumes control of the process. There are several automatic response systems for the online channel. They include

- Electronic pages with frequently asked questions (FAQs)
- Forms containing areas for suggestions, doubts, and complaints in the "Contact Us" section of a portal
- Virtual characters (avatars) with the ability to understand Internet user requests in their natural language, using technology based on artificial intelligence
- Programs that analyze e-mail message texts to direct the appropriate response content in a timely manner

Whether the response is automatic or requires human intervention, the database must always be updated so that it includes the history of all interactions with each individual. This information can help in future segmentation to create more precise campaigns. It is through the response channel that the company improves its knowledge of the target public's behavior. It can thus refine those parts of the program that require adjustment in order to develop an even closer relationship with its base.

Phase 2: Planning

This phase involves the detailed development of the communication plan for each segment of the base. This plan is made up of ranked marketing actions, with the goal of moving individuals to ever-higher relationship stages with the brand. This flow of actions must be designed in the utmost detail, identifying every possible response from the target public through the different online and offline channels. The program must be planned using the amount of time necessary for the final result to be aligned with the financial analysis that has been developed and with company expectations as a reference.

To illustrate the planning process, imagine a high-tech company that has a database of unknown individuals, a list amassed from several promotional events held during the calendar year. Its marketing professional believes that there are a large number of potential customers in this group and thus intends to develop a lead-generation program aimed at directing interested parties to the sales team, which, in turn, would carry out new transactions (see Figure 6.2). A possible detailed communication plan would involve the following steps:

1. Prequalification of the base's demographic information is done through the telemarketing channel to guarantee that data are up-to-date. The initial number of prospects is 100 individuals. The duration of the qualification action is 15 days.
2. Two new contact actions are implemented for the segment in which the first update attempt was not successful. Those individuals whose information was not confirmed after three attempts will be removed from the program. The number of nonqualified individuals is 6. The duration of the qualification action is 3 days.

Figure 6.2 Action Plan Workflow

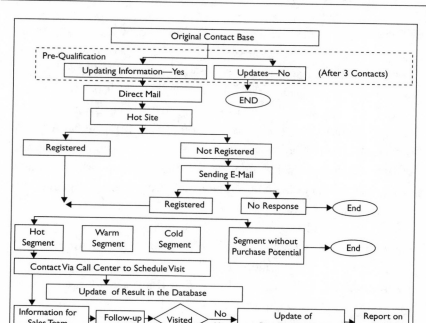

3. A direct mailing is sent to all the individuals with confirmed mailing addresses, offering a new product and requesting the interested parties to register at a specific site to schedule a visit by a representative. The Internet is used in this case because of the great interaction that technology professionals have with this channel. The number of direct mailings sent is 94. The number of registrations is 22. The duration of the registration action is 14 days.

4. An e-mail is sent to those individuals who did not register, highlighting the offer and again inviting them to visit the site. The number of e-mails sent is 72. The number of registrations is 6. The duration of the registration action is 4 days.

5. A form can identify each individual's purchasing potential and the urgency of a prospecting visit for each registered individual.

This will permit a more precise segmentation of the interested parties before directing them to sales representatives. The total number of individuals registered for immediate visits is 28.

6. Visits for the next two months are scheduled through a telemarketing operator. The number of scheduled visits is 18. The duration of the scheduling action is 10 days.

In this example, the complete program will last 46 days and has an 18 percent response rate from the original base. For each of the actions that is part of the complete solution, the operation time and returns should be estimated. Maximizing the program's general result means optimizing each of its parts, selecting the most appropriate channels in terms of the cost-benefit ratio.

If, as previously mentioned, the objective of the planning phase is to detail each communication action, the order of priority for developing the programs should also be established during this phase. The potential may be greater than the capacity for execution, as a result of resource limitations. Therefore, all options should be listed and ranked according to the importance of the criteria. The most relevant ones in the existing budget will be chosen. From this selection, it is possible to specify the action flow for each.

The analysis and planning phases together provide the formal specifications that describe in detail the strategy and corresponding tactics for implementing the relationship-marketing actions. At this point, it is important to observe that no piece has been developed and no creative component has been presented. The final result of these two phases is the elaboration of two documents called the functional design document (FDD) and the technical design document (TDD). The FDD describes in detail the actions to be developed for the respective segments. The TDD is an elaborated description of the necessary infrastructure, including the technology components and processes.

Phase 3: Implementation

The teams involved in developing communication pieces and program support infrastructure go into action based on the specifications in the functional and technical design documents. The
telemarketing company needs to develop the scripts for phone con-
versations. The direct-marketing agency begins the creation of
e-mail pieces, hot sites for the online channel, and direct mailings
for the offline channel. The media group chooses the vehicles to
use to disseminate the campaign and forwards the specifications
for the ads to be developed to the production team. The promotion agencies organize the events. Each program's database must
be designed with the necessary registries to precisely identify the
target public behavior. Maintenance and updating of registered
information must be implemented by a group with knowledge of
data services. A company specializing in developing analytical models is responsible for identifying behavioral patterns in the program's database in order to refine the marketing actions.

The implementation phase is managed by a multidisciplinary
group made up of professionals from several areas. This group
has the mission of making the relationship program defined in
the analysis and planning phases materialize. It is important that
this group be completely integrated. Indeed, this is one of the
most important responsibilities in this phase. Isolation of the
teams can result in a disjointed message and activities. Generally,
this occurs when tasks have been compartmentalized and when
management isn't centralized.

Compartmentalization occurs when the professionals involved
lack an overall view of the program and, as a consequence, fail to
understand the connections that exist between their participation
and that of others. It is important to have the involvement, even
if partial, of implementation groups during the analysis and planning phases. Jointly designed objectives and an overall vision of
the subsequent steps ensure everyone's commitment to an
integrated execution.

The centralized management issue is related to the need to control processes in a multidisciplinary environment made up of heterogeneous groups. The conventional model, in which several company professionals interact with several service providers, tends to generate development niches in which each group seeks to increase its participation in the solution without necessarily aligning its proposals with the program's main objectives. The role of a centralizing group is to put the focus on the brand's interests. This group is called the relationship integrator group or relationship manager, and it defines the scope of each team's work and controls the result, guaranteeing integration among all the parties (see Figure 6.3). It is critical that the relationship integrator group has profound knowledge of the different disciplines involved in order to arrive at the best solutions given the available funds. In some cases, the group is based on one or more professionals from inside the company. Other times, it may come from the relationship-marketing agency responsible for the program. However, most often this role is filled by a combination of company and agency professionals.

Phase 4: Control

The final phase of a relationship program encompasses comparing the results of the actions to the metrics estimated during the analysis phase. Value deviation, which is the difference between real and projected returns, is the quantitative representation of the adjustments necessary to align the two measurements. For example, if a demand-generation program has underestimated the number of new interested individuals, proportional investments should be added. If the income from a direct sales campaign has exceeded the planned goals, then part of the promotional budget could be suspended. Based on what was learned from the data resulting from this action, new ROI calculations will be made and used to guide future investments.

Figure 6.3 Relationship Integrator

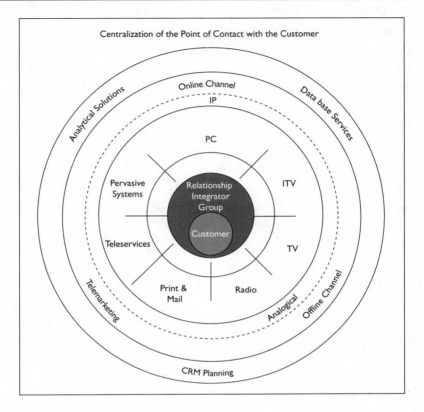

In order to analyze the results of the actions, you must measure the target public responses at every contact point with the
brand. This measurement should be handled in an individualized
manner, detailing how each person was affected by the communication. To do this, the control infrastructure must permit
recording of the base's behavioral data in computerized systems
that are made available at every existing channel. When direct
communication is used, implementation is natural. In the case of
the Internet, the environment lends itself to filing user activity in

a database. In telemarketing, the operators interact with specific software to store the history of the relationship with each individual. When it comes to direct-mail campaigns, the seed number concept is used, so that every addressee receives a piece with a different control number, enabling individualized follow-up of the responses. However, when mass communication, such as advertising and promotions, is used, the effectiveness of the action is measured by directing the receivers to measurable response channels through call-to-action techniques.

When all of these data-capturing systems are integrated, control of the response behavior is more comprehensive and permits a complete vision of the subject's interaction at different contact points. The more frequently this information is updated, the better the progress analysis of the program will be. The ideal situation is when the marketing professional can study the response pattern for the campaigns in real time, without needing to wait to take the necessary measures.

Key Points

- A relationship-marketing program should be structured in stages in order to guarantee the planned delivery of each of the parts. According to the Insight CRM methodology, created by Rapp Collins Brazil, implementation of such a program can be carried out in four phases: strategic analysis, planning, implementation, and control. In the first phase, we try to clearly identify the main objective of the marketing actions. This is the phase in which we define the target public we wish to reach, the marketing actions to be implemented and the most appropriate channels, the expected financial return, and the infrastructure required to support and execute the program. There are four main components in terms of infrastructure: a database, a relationship manager, fulfillment, and response channels.

- The second phase is planning, and it involves the detailed development of the communication plan for each segment of the base. Planning involves developing ordered marketing actions with the objective of transporting the individuals to ever-higher relationship stages with the brand. The analysis and planning phases together complete the formal specifications that describe in detail the strategy and corresponding tactics for implementing the relationship-marketing actions. At this point, no piece has been developed, and no creative component has been presented. The final result of these two phases is the creation of two documents called the functional design document (FDD) and the technical design document (TDD). The FDD describes in detail the actions to be developed for the respective segments. The TDD is an elaborated description of the necessary infrastructure, including the technology components and processes.
- The teams involved in developing communication pieces and program support infrastructure go into action based on the specifications from the FDD and the TDD.
- The final phase of a relationship program is called control, and it involves following up on the results of the actions to compare them to the metrics estimated in the analysis phase.

CHAPTER 7

Database Intelligence

D irect communication, a basic component of relationship marketing, is precise in its target. It selects individuals based on their propensity to respond. Then, it sends customized messages to the contact directions. And finally, it establishes a personalized channel to have a dialogue with the identified individuals. In each of these phases, the company gets individually acquainted with each member of the public, and it develops a different relationship with each participant, depending on the person's degree of interest in the brand.

The underlying principle is that different people behave differently and therefore require different offers. Their different needs are met by personalizing the message and the dialogue channel, which together develop the relationship between the individual and the company. From the moment that an individual shows interest in the brand, he or she should be monitored throughout the entire relationship cycle. Understanding individuals' preferences and behavior patterns is a critical factor in turning them into satisfied customers. The main objective of each implemented action should be to improve this relationship and raise it to higher levels.

To develop a closer relationship with the base, a company needs information about individual members of the target public in order to permit directed communication. The more complete the information, the better the chances of creating messages that will achieve the company's goals. Support from database systems is a basic condition for relationship-marketing programs to be implemented. The role of the database is not limited to the passive task of data storage. Its use is decisive in order to develop models that identify the most appropriate segments at which to aim campaigns.

We will now introduce the range of database features from a progressive perspective on their importance in implementing direct communication programs.

Phase 1: Basic Structure

What is the minimum amount of information required for a direct mailing? The name and address of the receiver. What is the minimum amount of information required for sending an e-mail? The name and e-mail address of the receiver. What is the minimum amount of information required to develop an active telemarketing action? The name and phone number of the receiver. In general, it is possible to develop the first direct communication actions using only the receiver's name and direction information.

One could argue that the receiver's address information would be sufficient. However, the creation of directed communication uses a minimum specification protocol based on permission marketing,[1] which states that the sender and the receiver of the message know each other and agree to begin a dialogue. In this case, using the receiver's name in the message confirms the necessary prerequisites while also empowering the communication with a personalized resource. The receiver recognizes that the message is directed individually to him or her and agrees to begin the process of interacting with the brand.

In this case, the required database is similar to a list that keeps only the two fields mentioned in each entry. Its structure is very simple, and its size will be directly proportional to the number of existing receivers.

Phase 2: Demographic Segmentation

The limitations of the previous model are the result of the small number of variables, which does not allow the target public to be described in any detail. If you have only the receivers' names and addresses, little can be done to elaborate a complete profile map of the base to help in the segmentation process. As a result, the only alternative is to treat the entire base uniformly, that is, not differentiate those who are potentially interested in an offer from those who have no interest at all. As a result, any communication action tends to have a lower response rate and a dubious rate of return on investment.

When the amount of information on each individual in the database is increased, the range of alternatives for segmentation increases significantly. With data on people's ages, it is possible to direct a promotion for sports cars at the younger brackets. If we know the individual's marital status, we can direct promotions for larger cars with plenty of cargo space at couples with more than two children. If we know people's income, we can aim ads for luxury cars only at those in the higher income brackets. As for companies that operate in business-to-business segments, other types of data could prove relevant, such as companies' location, number of employees, and earnings. Regardless of the market in which the company operates, there is a direct relationship between the target public's needs and its demographic data, which describe people's attributes or circumstances.

Relationship marketing seeks to explore this relationship, directing each communication action to groups with similar patterns. The database should keep the necessary data on each characteristic to permit the best segmentation. Technically, this is the equivalent of inserting new fields into the data table, which already contains name and direction information.

Phase 3: Psychographic and Behavioral Segmentation

Although demographics provide more data about the segmentation of the target public, sometimes this information is of limited value. For example, suppose we are looking for people who are interested in extreme sports. Which of these variables would best describe this profile: name, gender, or address? Rarely would any of these help identify the desired individuals.

Consider using psychographic information to gain a fuller picture of the base. Those data would include people's interests, activities, and values. For example, some people like antique cars, whereas others are more interested in wearing the latest fashion. Some participate in certain leisure activities, such as tennis, while others prefer reading. As for identifying people's values, there are several types of communities. Environmentalists, for instance, advocate protecting natural resources as a way to achieve a more balanced ecosystem. Pacifists push for an end to wars and aggression. When we know our contact base's psychographic portrait, we have a better chance of presenting an appropriate offer. When crafting an effective message about sports travel vacations, it is much more helpful to know that a group of people enjoys radical sports than to know the city in which they live.

We should fill in as many fields in the database as necessary to save the new information on our target public. The objective is to build a solution that will enable us to gain detailed knowledge of the base and then identify several segments of people with similar behavior patterns.

Once the communication campaigns are sent to the different groups, we should also save each individual's responses in the database. Who purchased the offer, who declared moderate interest, and who provided no response whatsoever? This category of information adds a new dimension to the data quality. We have begun to save the base's true behavior. While the demographic and psychographic profiles help us to design better campaigns, the behavior attribute reflects the result we achieved. By analyzing the responses relative to the conjectures made, we can fine-tune our knowledge of the contact base and thus improve future communications.

Phase 4: Integration with the Legacy and Other Systems

Being able to fill the database with the relevant data is not a simple task. In many cases, the company's marketing department does not have all the information needed. It is necessary to search other sources for missing material in order to develop a complete picture of the base. There are several possibilities. The first is to look in the company's other databases. Transactional information, which describes how each individual spends money, can be found in the financial database. It includes the answers to the following questions:

- What is each individual's average purchase volume?
- How often does the person engage in transactions?
- What is the person's preferred means of payment?
- How many installments does he or she normally opt for?
- What was the date of the last order?

Information related to satisfaction can be found in the customer service database. It includes the answers to the following questions:

- What are the most frequent complaints?
- What is the most used type of support?
- With what frequency has the person used these services?

Information about people's registration or demographic data could be more up to date in the company's sales database than in its marketing database. And psychographic information can be found in the Internet database, which recovers important data on the base's interests through surveys.

To integrate the relationship-marketing database with the company's traditional systems requires automatically feeding data recovered from other points of contact into the relationship program. In this phase, it is important to consider the validation of migration rules that guarantee the consistency of the new information. The content recovered from the legacy systems should feed the relationship base without compromising the existing structure. Duplicate data should be removed to ensure that you don't have two registries with conflicting information. Standardization, in turn, requires the support of a data dictionary to establish specifications for all existing fields, such as accepted titles (Dr. Ms., etc.), maximum size of valid addresses, specifications for zip code descriptions, and formulas to calculate the control digit in verification algorithms.

When the necessary information is not available, some companies have resorted to telemarketing tactics. Trained operators contact the interest base and ask the individuals to answer some questions to fill out the database. Although this practice is common, its main limitations are that it inconveniences individuals, interrupting them at home or at work, and that it tends to be expensive.

Renting or buying external lists is an alternative way to fill out the base attributes. For the consumer market, these lists can be supplied by magazine subscription companies, associations or clubs, and credit card companies. For the corporate market, there are many companies that specialize in providing lists with information for several industry and service categories. It is possible to identify which entries in the external list have the same people as those in the base list by using a procedure known as data matching. Additional and more up-to-date data will correct previously collected information.

Regardless of how data are acquired, the work involved in guaranteeing the execution of their integration cannot be underestimated. Incomplete information makes it impossible to fully develop base segmentation, which is the foundation upon which the entire relationship program should be structured.

Phase 5: Keeping Data Updated

Database content is perpetually in need of upkeep. People change jobs and move. They marry, separate, and have more children. Companies have different earning levels, and their human resources are reallocated to other departments. According to a survey by Target Marketing,[2] the average update rate for company databases is 2 percent per month, and for the consumer market, it is 4 percent per month. That means that approximately every four and two years, respectively, all existing data in the database lose their validity!

Keeping customers' information accurate is a basic condition for developing relationship programs. Data that aren't updated have several negative implications. On one side, they generate inaccurate segmentations. As a result, there is a lower likelihood of response from communication campaigns. What is the impact of creating a daring direct sales action for DVD players for a group of people that enjoys watching movies and has only TVs? Probably high. What happens when the information about the equipment each individual owns is outdated and some already own DVD players? The responses will probably be much lower.

Sometimes, incorrect fields do not allow the communication to reach its target. How will international tourists who enjoy traveling react to a promotion for Carnival in Rio de Janeiro, Brazil? Probably favorably. What happens when the addresses for some of the people in the group are outdated? If some of them have moved over the past few months, what are the chances that this communication will achieve the expected results? If an address is incorrect, the message will never reach its destination, and regardless of how good the offer may be or how appropriate it is for the target public, this minor detail makes it impossible to get a response from potentially interested individuals.

In addition to the problems related to the segmentation and fulfillment processes, outdated information compromises the company's brand. Receiving a promotion for a new car when you are still an adolescent reflects a complete lack of knowledge concerning your age. Sending a catalog for baby products to a single person causes surprise. Offering an additional credit card through a telemarketing action, while at the same time denying an increase in the first card's limit at the bank, is at the very least confusing to the customer. In such cases, breaks in dialogue continuity occur. The fragility of the interaction becomes evident, compromising the evolution of the relationship between the company and its target public.

The ways in which a company can keep its data updated are similar to the methods employed to enter new information in the database, which were discussed in the previous section. First, the company can use active telemarketing: call the contact base and ask people to corroborate information and correct what is no longer accurate. This strategy must be used with caution in order not to tire the contact base with an extensive questionnaire. We can also resort to gathering more recent information from other company databases, such as the Internet and financial, and customer service databases. Finally, we can analyze the individuals' responses in the marketing campaigns and control incorrect addressing (nixies) in fulfillment actions.

It is essential to enter the updated information without delay. Time lags between the recovery of correct data and correcting the information in the database can mean the difference between an individual who is disappointed and one who is satisfied with the communication received.

Phase 6: Transforming Information into Knowledge

It is critical that base information include complete demographic, psychographic, and behavioral data, as we discussed in the previous sections. It is also indispensable that the information be up-to-date, reflecting the base's current living situation. It is possible to create appropriate segmentations that permit identifying groups with similar behavior to enable future communication actions using these existing attributes. Two main questions arise:

- How can we develop segmentations that represent the different categories of the customer base?
- What process should we use to select the qualities that reflect each consumer's unique attitudes and needs?

In general, segmentation begins with the building of super-groups. In other words, the first grouping level, the one with the most general relevant information, is the set of individuals with similar needs. For example, if we take a company that sells computers, we could have large corporate customers, small corporate customers, government, and end users.

Additional factors that are specific to each supergroup should then be considered. It is not necessary for these factors to be the same. Furthermore, within a group, some traits could be more relevant than others. This requires dividing each group into brackets, with additional details being necessary for such a division. In the previous example, the group of large corporate customers can be further divided into those with high, average, and low lifetime value (LTV).

The concept of information density is another consideration involved in the segmentation process. This term refers to the number of interactions each individual has with the brand. Some people use several channels to gain access to several company products. Others limit themselves to a single product and a single channel. The variations between these two extremes describe the existing levels of public information density. When this number is high, it indicates better opportunities to describe people and consequently chart their interests and needs. In our example, we can also segment the subgroup of large corporate customers with high LTV into those that consume a single product and those that consume products in several different categories, such as servers and desktops.

Precisely identifying the traits and needs of individuals who mirror a particular behavior pattern is not an easy task. For example, the color a customer chooses when buying a car can be a characteristic that helps differentiate one group from another, but it is not necessarily a determining factor in buying. In other words, even if one group gives priority to buying blue cars and another to buying black ones, the "car color" factor is not necessarily a determining factor in purchasing the vehicle.

The most common way to determine the connection between attitude and behavior is through surveys and focus groups with a sample of the target public. Using specific questions, you can glean each group's needs and motivations. The idea that a questionnaire needs to be lengthy and detailed to capture all the desired information is a fallacy. Indeed, it is impossible to ask everything. Specificity is the key to obtaining relevant results.

To choose the most appropriate questions for these surveys, start by analyzing the existing behavioral data. In order to choose the correct attitude variables, it is vital to explore the different groups of customers and their purchasing habits. You will need to develop hypotheses about the needs and motivations driving different consumers' behaviors.

Statistical models based on regression techniques[3] are built from the responses in order to identify the most significant correlations between the set of selected variables and the corresponding behavior patterns.

In those cases in which there is a high correlation with the sample selected, the model should be applied to the rest of the base with the same characteristics. The supposition that the sample chosen is representative permits you to extrapolate the knowledge acquired to the group being represented. Corresponding marketing campaigns are directed to those segments in which there is strong mathematical proof that the individuals will respond positively.

The creation of models is the main objective of the process that seeks to transform database information into knowledge. Finding customer profiles that will respond similarly to a communication campaign is like rummaging through all the existing data and finding the hidden meaning buried in their values. According to Novo,[4] in order to find the patterns that describe the behavior of the target public, it is necessary to understand the data language. Once a company finds out that female consumers have a greater tendency to shop on weekends, the firm can develop programs that focus on Saturday and Sunday promotions. If you identify a pattern, such as that male consumers who are 30 to 45 years old and buy blue sports coats also have a higher probability of purchasing white shirts, that makes it easier to create a directed communication for this group by highlighting the merchandise of interest. Likewise, knowing that your most valuable customers are not purchasing new versions of your technology products because of the difficulty they are having in installing new systems is vital for you so that you can concentrate your resources on support services.

To see an example of an application based on consumer segmentation to maximize returns on communication actions, consult the appendix, "Insights on Customers through Segmentation: Study in the Wireless Telecommunications Sector."

Companies use several different models to prepare their marketing proposals. Each one is adapted to fit its specific situation and objectives. The RFM model (recency, frequency, and monetary value) identifies the customers who have made recent purchases, that is, those with the greatest likelihood of responding to marketing actions. The response and earnings model identifies the customers or potential customers with the greatest likelihood of generating the highest earnings in a marketing program. The propensity model identifies the group of products that the consumer is most likely to buy. The antiattrition model points out those customers who are most likely to leave the brand and replace it with another. The purchase time model identifies those customers who have not had any commercial transactions with the company for some time, signaling an increased risk of abandonment.

In order to maximize the result of communication campaigns, using the database as a technology that transcends data storage is a must. These databases need to be transformed into knowledge to allow specific segments of consumers to be addressed using campaigns that are relevant to their needs and their behaviors. Companies that use the information they have obtained in an efficient manner, whether they obtained it through their own registries, navigation on Internet sites, online and offline transactions, or external lists, can maximize the return on their investments. The benefit from allocating resources correctly increases substantially when this strategy is systematically used for marketing decisions.

Key Points

- The more complete and individualized the information you have about the target public, the better your chances of creating personalized messages that achieve your marketing objectives. As a result, it is essential to have the support of database systems to implement relationship programs. Their roles are not limited to data storage. They are decisive in developing models that link the most appropriate segments to the most appropriate campaigns. Their basic structures include information about the receivers' name and address. With this information alone, it is possible to develop the first direct communication actions, although the results are likely to be modest because of the paucity of information describing the target public. You go up another step by adding data such as age, marital status, and income, permitting a demographic segmentation of the base. In order to have a more complete view, the next step is to consider psychographic material such as interests, activities, and personal values.

- Once messages are sent to the different groups, make sure to save each individual's responses in the database. While the demographic and psychographic attributes help in developing more effective campaigns, the behavioral data reflect the result actually achieved.
- Information is often still lacking, and it becomes necessary to search for it in other sources. The first option is to look in the company's other databases. To integrate the relationship program with the company's legacy systems requires automatically feeding the data recovered from other points of contact into the relationship program. Other ways to track down information include telemarketing actions and renting or buying external lists.
- Regardless of how the data are acquired, it is essential to keep them updated. Furthermore, the material needs to be transformed into knowledge in order to provide insights that will allow you to create targeted campaigns that will be relevant to different segments of consumers. Companies that use the information they gather efficiently and effectively can maximize the return on their marketing investments.

CHAPTER 8

Financial Analysis: The Unquestionable Proof of the Results

In order to improve communication actions, above all, it is necessary to have a precise understanding of the quantitative results. How can we increase the number of responses we get from a lead-generation campaign if we do not know for certain how many interested parties responded to the message? How can we create more effective programs to recover customers if we don't know how many individuals were recovered through our actions?

Having the ability to measure the results of a marketing campaign is a necessary precondition for systematically developing practices that will continuously improve return on investment.

To measure does not mean to observe what people say they want or will do. It means to record real responses in real situations. By using the call-to-action technique shown in Chapters 4 and 5, we immediately know if the interest was translated into a real response from the target public. It is possible to follow up on the behavior of interested parties and measure their actions in the form of phone calls, clicks on e-mails, or the return of response cards. When response numbers are low, it is important to learn from the mistake. Isolate the various parts of the message and test new alternatives. On the other hand, when response numbers are high, this establishes benchmarks for future campaigns.

There are several metrics to choose from. These are defined in the strategic analysis phase of communication programs, as described in Chapter 6, and together with investment financial information, they make up the key performance indicators (KPI) in communication campaigns.

In this chapter, we will introduce the procedures for analyzing the financial return on investments in relationship-marketing programs.

Customer Value Increment

Before they can try to maximize returns on a specific communication action, companies must plot the marketing investments required to ensure continuous gains in profitability. Which actions should be given priority? What kinds of resources should be allocated to each? The answers to these questions are determined by the relationship between the investments and the different profiles of existing customers in the contact base. The largest resource allocations should occur in situations where the individuals' customer behaviors will be altered, increasing their lifetime values (LTV) and, consequently, the company's cash flow and investor wealth. Or, more specifically, investments should be made only for those consumers where additional LTV gains exceed costs.

When interactions between the company and its customers are recorded, the firm can link earnings and costs for each customer and thus calculate individual LTV increases. As a result, customers can be ranked according to incremental values of profitability. Then, communications are applied to individuals with the most expressive returns.

According to Behram Hansotia,[1] for each investment opportunity based on incremental maximization criteria for LTV, a communication program should be developed and tested and the economic performance should be analyzed for future actions. Pilot campaigns are elaborated with a representative sample of

Figure 8.1 The Consumer Value Increment Process

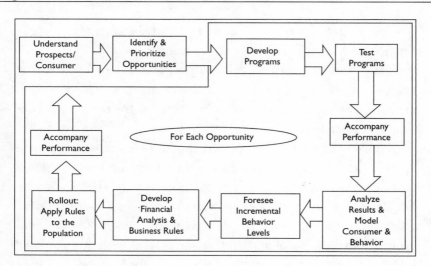

the target public before the action is applied to the entire population. This process, called the consumer value increment, can be represented as shown in Figure 8.1.

The process is based on the learning curve. With each new cycle, greater knowledge of the actions being employed is used to create new and even more effective campaigns. The financial analysis, based on how a sample of the population performed, enables companies to cancel programs with low rates of return before they've been developed into full-fledged campaigns aimed at the entire target public. Consequently, the costs of testing communication campaigns are entirely justifiable, and the expenses are offset by the campaigns' contributions to future profits.

We will now look at the procedures necessary to obtain the financial details on communication actions. The main objective of this analysis is to calculate the return on marketing investment, or ROMI (also known simply as return on investment, or ROI) for the various existing opportunities so that professionals can make decisions on resource allocations based on quantitative indicators.

Financial Analysis

According to Shepard,[2] two situations must be considered in the financial analysis of communication campaigns.

The first is called front-end analysis, and it is focused on the acquisition of new customers. The second is called back-end analysis, and it is related to actions directed at the company's current customer base.

Acquisition actions are more costly than maintenance actions. As we saw in Chapter 3, companies need to invest more to win a new customer than to keep that customer loyal. Therefore, why not devote all marketing resources strictly to relationship programs with the current base? Since the consumer life cycle will eventually reach the abandonment stage, it is necessary to make up for the quantitative decrease. Otherwise, the business will wane and ultimately disappear. Since the acquisition of customers is necessary, the ability to balance the costs of acquiring a new customer with his or her LTV is a basic condition for the company to be able to grow over the long term.

There are two types of acquisition programs: those whose objective is to profit from a single action (with such programs, the return must pay the costs of the action and still generate the projected margin), and those where the acquisition campaign is only the first step in developing programs that generate continuous cash flows for the company (in this case, the first transaction is the beginning of a long-term relationship with the objective of generating repeated purchases). If the profit or loss from this action is excluded from LTV calculations, it can be interpreted as an investment.

There are various examples of product categories that use the latter strategy. In the end user segment, there are telephone, Internet, video rental, and bookstore companies. In the B2B segment, there are consulting firms and technology companies, to name a few.

The logic that supports the two types of acquisition programs—the programs based on a single order and the programs supported by continuous cash flows—determines the relationship between the resources required and the expectations for return on investments. Programs aimed at a single transaction require a lower initial investment, and their short-term returns are greater. However, these advantages will be sustained over the long term only if the company is able to maintain business frequency. On the other hand, long-term programs aimed at developing continuity relationships have lower rates of return in the initial stages, but they guarantee the frequency of cash flows throughout the entire relationship cycle. To project future rates of return, add up the cash flows from all customers. In this case, the planning of marketing actions can be developed from financial information that is more precise than that found in single-order actions.

The Cost Component

The costs of marketing action can be represented by the cost per thousand (CPM) indicator, which shows the investment needed to develop communication actions by using a sample of 1,000 people as a reference.

$$\text{CPM} = \frac{\text{cost of action} \times 1,000}{\text{number of people reached}}$$

For illustrative purposes, let's imagine that it costs \$5,000 to send a direct-mail piece to 100,000 people. The CPM value is

$$\text{CPM} = \frac{5,000 \times 1,000}{100,000}$$

$$\text{CPM} = \$50$$

That means that to reach 1,000 people with this action, the total investment required is $50.

The CPM should be calculated for all communication actions in the several contact channels with the consumer. The various components that make up the cost structure must be considered in each case. For example, in direct-mail actions, the following items should be considered: printing, rental or acquisition of a list, label processing, shipping and handling, creation, art, and production of the piece. In e-mail marketing actions, the most important costs are the rental or acquisition of the list, sending, art, and production. In order to develop telemarketing actions, it is necessary to calculate communication script elaboration costs, rental or acquisition of the list when active actions are involved, contact operators, control supervisor, and a technological structure made up of phone lines, hardware, and software. In advertising, the CPM calculation involves media costs and the creation and production of the ad.

There are fixed-cost components in every channel, and they need to be allocated regardless of the number of pieces sent, the number of telemarketing operators used, or the circulation of the vehicle. These include monthly payments to the relationship-marketing agency and the expenses for assembling the operational structure. The values for these expenses that are added to the final CPM calculation for each action should be proportional to the sums used. On the other hand, variable costs are highly dependent on the size of the action. The CPM for printing a letter for 10,000 people is higher than it is for printing a letter for 1,000,000 people. Therefore, it is expected that the actions that reach the largest number of people will have the lowest CPM.

CPM is a cost indicator that permits an analysis of the optimal allocation of financial resources given the available alternatives. It can be used to identify the vehicle with the best proposal when elaborating media planning. For example, comparing the CPMs for the online channel and for telemarketing when structuring response channels in lead-generation campaigns helps companies choose the lowest-cost alternative.

The Response Component

It is not enough to identify the lowest cost for an action; we must also analyze the number of responses obtained. Lower-cost actions often result in low returns as well. Response percentage (R%) and response per thousand (RPM) are the indicators used in relationship-marketing campaigns to measure response results. The first establishes the ratio between the total number of responses and the number of people reached. The second uses the same ratio for a base of 1,000 people.

$$R\% = \frac{\text{number of responses} \times 100}{\text{number of people reached}}$$

$$RPM = \frac{\text{number of responses} \times 1,000}{\text{number of people reached}}$$

or

$$RPM = R\% \times 10$$

For example, let's suppose that of 50,000 people who received an e-mail marketing piece aimed at getting them to register their information on a hot site, 10,000 people filled out the necessary data. The response percentage for this action is 20 percent, and the number of responses per thousand is 200:

$$R\% = \frac{10,000 \times 100}{50,000}$$

$$RPM = \frac{10,000 \times 1,000}{50,000}$$

Cost per Response Component

The combined use of the CPM and RPM indicators enables marketing professionals to measure the cost per response, or CPR, for each communication action:

$$CPR = \frac{CPM}{RPM}$$

The cost per response indicator permits a comparison among the different alternatives by standardizing the data. The main challenge for the marketing professional is to identify the most effective communication parameters to minimize CPR values. These can range from the creative variables discussed in Chapter 5 to the selection of the most appropriate vehicles and channels.

For purposes of illustration, let's imagine that $200,000 is available for developing a lead-generation program and that the available channel alternatives to catch people's attention are direct mail, telemarketing, e-mail marketing, and print advertising with call to action. The estimated CPM and response percentage for each channel is shown in Tables 8.1 and 8.2. In this case, the most important thing is to identify the best alternative for investment considering the available resources. Or, in other words, to find the available option that maximizes the number of qualified responses.

Starting with the total budget for the campaign, it is possible to identify the action's maximum coverage in each channel. The funds available for direct mail cover the cost for creating, producing,

Table 8.1 CPM Value for Each Channel

Budget Available: $ 200,000.00

Channel	CPM (in $)
Direct Mail	10,000
E-mail Marketing	1,000
Telemarketing	8,000
Print Ads	400

Table 8.2 Data for Choosing the Maximum Response Channel

Budget Available: $ 200,000.00

Channel	Response Percentage (R%)
Direct Mail	2.5 percent
E-mail Marketing	0.2 percent
Telemarketing	1.0 percent
Print Ads	0.02 percent

and sending 20,000 pieces. This number grows to 200,000 pieces in the case of e-mail marketing. Active telemarketing can reach 25,000 different people, whereas print advertising can be included in a magazine that goes out to 500,000 readers.

At first glance, print advertising seems to be the most advantageous channel, since it reaches more people. However, to confirm these suspicions, it is necessary to use CPR calculations. The next step (see Table 8.3) involves calculating the responses per thousand, or RPM, for each channel by simply multiplying the R% values found in Table 8.2 by 10.

Finally, by calculating the cost per response value in each channel as the quotient of the CPM and the RPM, we arrive at the result for the simulation. See Table 8.4.

Table 8.3 RPM Value for Each Channel

Budget Available: $ 200,000.00

Channel	RPM
Direct Mail	25
E-mail Marketing	2
Telemarketing	10
Print Ads	0.2

Table 8.4 CPR Value per Channel

Budget Available: $ 200,000.00

Channel	CPR
Direct Mail	400
E-mail Marketing	500
Telemarketing	800
Print Ads	2,000

Direct mail, which has the lowest CPR value, initially seemed to be the least qualified because of its higher cost per thousand, but in reality it is the channel that generates the best result. It reaches 500 individuals for the $200,000 investment, whereas e-mail marketing, telemarketing, and advertising reach 400, 250, and 100, respectively.

When campaigns have two or more steps, calculate the CPR by using the sum of the necessary investments in each of the phases and the final number of effectively converted consumers. For example, in a direct-sales campaign, the program can be planned as the concatenation of two complementary actions: a direct mailing that directs the interested parties to a call center number, where the attendant can take the final order. The investment in the direct-mail action should be added to the cost of the receptive telemarketing action to obtain the total amount of resources necessary for developing the program. The total number of converted individuals—that is, those who effectively purchased the offer—corresponds to the total coverage of the public from the first action multiplied by the response percentage (R%) in each of the subsequent phases. In a general sense, the CPR for programs with n steps can be represented by the following equation:

$$CRP = \frac{\sum_{1}^{n} \text{investment}}{\text{initial scope} \times \prod_{1}^{n} R\%}$$

In this example, if the direct-mail action had a cost of $5,000 and a 2.0 percent response rate, for a public of 100,000 people, and the call center action needs an investment of $1,000 for a 1.0 percent response, the final CPR value is $300:

$$CPR = \frac{5,000 + 1,000}{100,000 \times 0.02 \times 0.01} = 300$$

Return on Investment

Maximizing the number of responses in a communication action is just part of the financial analysis process. Its complement involves measuring the return on investment. This is the ratio between the campaign's contribution to profits and the sum of the resources necessary to develop the campaign.

$$ROI = \frac{\text{profit}}{\text{investment}}$$

In order to calculate the ROI for a communication action, the profit variable should be measured by subtracting cost of sales, created program costs, and necessary overhead costs from gross sales. In the case of a product company, the cost of sales involves items such as product cost, order processing, shipping, handling, and special discounts that are applied at times.

For illustration purposes, let's imagine an active telemarketing campaign for 10,000 people that seeks the direct sale of a product with a margin of $120.00. In this case, the merchandise, transportation, storage, fulfillment, and overhead costs associated with computer, financial, and support personnel have already been subtracted from the product price. If the action's response percentage is 1.0 percent and the total costs related to overhead and promotion are a $4,000 fixed component and a $0.50 variable component per individual receiving the communication, the corresponding ROI calculation will be

$$
\begin{aligned}
\text{Total gross margin} &= \text{target public} \times \text{response percentage} \times \\
&\qquad \text{product margin} \\
&= 10{,}000 \times 0.01 \times 120 \\
&= 12{,}000
\end{aligned}
$$

$$
\begin{aligned}
\text{Total campaign cost} &= \text{fixed cost} + \text{variable cost} \\
&= 4{,}000 + (10{,}000 \times 0.5) \\
&= 9{,}000
\end{aligned}
$$

$$
\begin{aligned}
\text{Profit} &= \text{total gross margin} - \text{total campaign cost} \\
&= 3{,}000
\end{aligned}
$$

$$
\text{ROI} = \frac{\text{profit}}{\text{total campaign cost}}
$$

$$
= \frac{3{,}000}{9{,}000} = 33.33\%
$$

Table 8.5 ROI Values for Different Sizes of Target Public and Different Response Percentages

R%/Population	0.5%	1.0%	1.5%	2.0%	3.0%	4.0%
1,000	−86.67%	−73.33%	−60.00%	−46.67%	−20.00%	6.67%
2,000	−76.00%	−52.00%	−28.00%	−4.00%	44.00%	92.00%
3,000	−67.27%	−34.55%	−1.82%	30.91%	96.36%	161.82%
4,000	−60.00%	−20.00%	20.00%	60.00%	140.00%	220.00%
5,000	−53.85%	−7.69%	38.46%	84.62%	208.57%	269.23%
6,000	−48.57%	2.86%	54.29%	105.71%	208.57%	311.43%
7,000	−44.00%	12.00%	68.00%	124.00%	236.00%	348.00%
8,000	−40.00%	20.00%	80.00%	140.00%	260.00%	380.00%
9,000	−36.47%	27.06%	90.59%	154.12%	281.18%	408.24%
10,000	−33.33%	33.33%	100.00%	166.67%	300.00%	433.33%

We now show Table 8.5 with the ROI values for different sizes of the target public with response percentages ranging from 0.5 percent to 4 percent. The highlighted cells correspond to positive ROI values.

Some conclusions can be drawn from the analysis of these numbers. As expected, increasing response percentage values for a constant target public size have a positive impact on ROI values. This happens as a result of the profit increment after the increase in sales without the corresponding impact on the cost curve.

Some ROI values are negative. In these cases, the costs of developing the action are higher than the return it brings. As discussed earlier, unless the action is developed to acquire new customers with positive LTVs that justify the investment, campaigns with negative ROI should not be implemented. Calculating the value at which ROI is null, or the breakeven point at which campaign profit is also null, is similar to finding the number of positive responses for which total gross margin equals the marketing contribution, that is, the total cost for the campaign. The result is calculated by the ratio between total campaign cost and total gross margin.

$$\begin{array}{c}\text{Number of products}\\ \text{required for breakeven}\end{array} = \frac{\text{total campaign cost}}{\text{total gross margin}}$$

In the simulated telemarketing action, the total number of products required is

$$\begin{array}{c}\text{Number of products}\\ \text{required for breakeven}\end{array} = \frac{9,000}{120} = 75$$

Since the actual number of products sold was 100 (the public times the response percentage), 25 products beyond the breakeven quota corresponded to the campaign's positive profit after marketing contribution. The response percentage that corresponds to the breakeven rate is calculated by dividing the number of products required for breakeven by the size of the target public.

$$\text{R\%} = \frac{75}{10,000} = 0.75\%$$

The response percentages that correspond to the breakeven rates for the target public between 1,000 and 10,000 people in the simulated action are shown in Table 8.6.

To maximize ROI values, it is often better for the professional to choose campaigns with a smaller target base that also have a higher response percentage. Even if the total sales volume and profits decrease, it is possible to have a higher return on the investment.

Table 8.5 shows that an action for 2,000 people with a 3 percent response generates an ROI of 44 percent, higher than the 33.33 percent from the previous simulation. Observe that in the first case, the number of products sold is 60, less than the 100 products sold in the previous situation. The absolute profit is also

Table 8.6 Variations in Breakeven Rates

Population	Breakeven Rate
1,000	3.75%
2,000	2.08%
3,000	1.53%
4,000	1.25%
5,000	1.08%
6,000	0.97%
7,000	0.89%
8,000	0.83%
9,000	0.79%
10,000	0.75%

lower. While the absolute profit in the action with a 1.0 percent response is $3,000, in the simulation with a 3.0 percent response, this sum falls to $2,200. On the other hand, campaign costs also decrease with a smaller base, and at a faster rate than income.

The company should make the choice in favor of higher ROIs, sometimes at the expense of lower sales volumes. However, the ideal situation is when actions with high ROIs can be applied consecutively. In such cases, the company is able to simultaneously enjoy high rates of return, sales, and profit.

ROI rates must be calculated using a standard time unit that permits a comparison between the different campaign alternatives. If one action has an ROI of 90 percent for a three-year period and another has a 70 percent return for two years, when calculated on an annual basis, they are 30 percent and 35 percent, respectively. The second option is more advantageous in financial terms.

Relationship-marketing campaigns are supported by analysis instruments, with the objective of planning the best allocation of resources. The measurement of each action's results permits the comparison of estimated values with those that were actually achieved, thus serving as a reference to improve future communications. This refining process is progressive. Using the financial analysis of cost, response, and ROI components, the marketing professional can pinpoint the weakest points in the communication actions and devote the necessary resources to maximizing the intended returns.

Key Points

- In order to increase the performance of communication actions, it is necessary to fully grasp the quantitative results. The ability to measure marketing campaign results is a basic requirement for systematically developing practices that will continuously improve returns on investments. By measuring each action's results, you can compare estimated values with those actually achieved and thus gain a reference point for improving future communications. There are several metrics to choose from.
- The costs can be represented by the cost per thousand (CPM) indicator, which shows the investment needed to develop communication actions. CPM makes it possible to analyze the optimal financial allocation of resources given the available options. However, merely identifying the lowest cost for an action is not enough; we must also analyze the number of responses obtained. Lower-cost actions often result in low returns as well.
- Response percentage (R%) or response per thousand (RPM) is the indicator used to measure response results. The first establishes the ratio between the total number of responses and the number of people reached. The second uses the same ratio for a base of 1,000 people. The combined use of the CPM and RPM indicators enables the marketing

professional to measure the cost per response, or CPR, for each communication action.

- The use of CPR permits comparing the different communication alternatives through a standardization of data. Maximizing the number of responses in a communication action is just part of the financial analysis process. Its complement involves measuring the return on investment (ROI), which is the ratio between the contribution to profits and the sum of the resources necessary to develop the campaign.
- Using the financial analysis of cost, response, and ROI, the marketing professional can gain an understanding of the weakest points in the communication actions and decide how to allocate resources based on quantitative indicators aimed at maximizing returns.

CHAPTER 9

Successful Cases

In this chapter, we present case studies in which relationship marketing was used by a wide range of product and service companies in the consumer and business-to-business markets. This section has two purposes. The first is to illustrate how major global brands have successfully used this technique as part of their portfolio of communication options. The results of campaigns will be described whenever possible. The second goal is to help marketing professionals gain new insights into their needs.

We selected case studies involving companies in North America, Latin America, and Europe to demonstrate the global scope of relationship marketing. All of the case studies were based on clients of Rapp Collins agencies. This group has a high profile in the world of direct communication. Founded 35 years ago, Rapp Collins has a network of more than 50 offices in 47 countries and has developed an enormous number of communication campaigns throughout its history.

The cases are presented in the following format: the "background" provides the context, the situation in which the company found itself when the communication need was identified; the "challenge" lays out the problem; the "solution" describes the relationship-marketing strategy that was applied to overcome the challenge; and the "results" show what happened after the solution was applied.

Note: disclosure of all the cases presented here was authorized by the clients. In some situations, information related to the results was omitted to preserve customer secrecy (NDA).

Case 1: Air France—France

Loyalty Program

Agency: Rapp Collins France

Background
Air France and KLM decided to join forces and their destinies to build a *new entity that would be on a par with the great European market*. A guiding principle for the merger was that this would be one group made up of two airline companies, each of which would retain its brand, its identity, and its culture.

Challenge
In April 2005, Air France-KLM developed a common loyalty program. This was the first time two leading European companies had merged their loyalty programs to create a single one. The major challenges were to demonstrate the benefits of the merger to travelers and emphasize local client satisfaction, capture and generate more value, and reduce costs. This was an enormous challenge right from the start, since there were 10 million members at the time the program was launched, €3.7 billion turnover was generated by the program, and 26.4 percent of passenger turnover was within the new group.

Solution
The solution was based on three main strategies (see Figures 9.1 to 9.6):

1. Develop a communication territory specific to the loyalty program. The strategic choice was to be educational, bringing concrete proof that the program delivers more: more opportunities for miles, more awards, and easier access to higher levels of rewards. At the time of launch, the message was generosity. The communication was

Figure 9.1 Flying Blue Welcome Pack. Promise: "The best of the first European program only for you."

Figure 9.2 Recurrent Card Renewal Campaign. Send out the new card with an incentive to visit the dedicated Flying Blue Web site.

Figure 9.3 Home Page of the Flying Blue Dedicated Web Site.

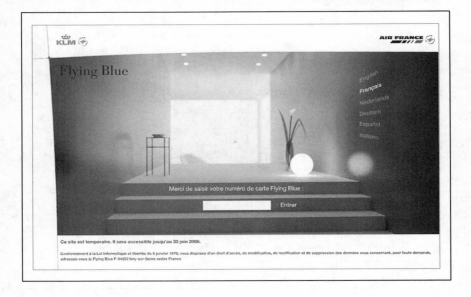

Figure 9.4 Personalized Space According to Card Level.

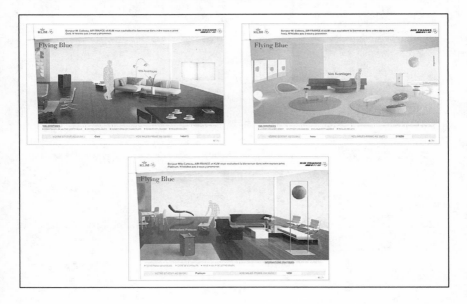

Figure 9.5 Illustration—Program Life-Cycle Communications. Bimonthly newsletters.

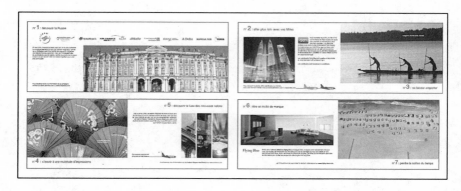

Figure 9.6 Illustration—Client Life-Cycle Communications. Activation operation.

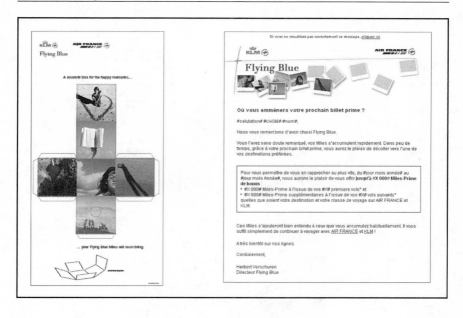

determined by the different membership levels within the program. Once the new program rules were explained, then it was stressed that consumers were members of one of the most attractive and biggest programs on the market. "Refresh the way you experience travel," was the slogan.

2. Decrease investments while seeking to stress the quality of the relationship and the program's performance. The goal here was to generate more business and relationship value with the same budget, while recruiting and managing more members. This was done by redirecting investments based on their business potential and risks, and by engaging in a proactive push for program e-change. This meant considering online as a tool to enrich the relationship with the traveler, systematically changing links from off to on, and developing recurrent e-qualification operations such as self-promotion banners on Air France sites and specific e-mail campaigns.

3. Develop relationship orchestration based on three cycles: the program life cycle, the client life cycle, and a cycle linked to specific market changes. In the first case, the goal was to develop attachment and create the consumer reflex. This was done by mileage summaries, newsletters, market-specific inserts, and a renewal and welcome process. In the second case, the goal was to maintain and stimulate airline activity. The communication was based on miles or discount offers through punctual or recurring operations. In the third case, the goal was to support market-specific sales objectives. This was accomplished through miles or discount offers via ad hoc communications.

Results

After 300 days of the program, the results were:

1. The number of members increased from 10 to 11.2 million, an increase of 12 percent.
2. The program member activity rate grew from 44 percent to 58 percent.

3. Turnover decreased from 8.1 percent to 6.8 percent.
4. There was a true e-change success, with
   - 4,300,000 qualified member e-mails
   - 38.8 percent qualified members
   - 85 percent of clients with higher card levels receiving all or part of their communication online
5. Despite the merger context, the costs invested by asset have been rationalized by 2.5 percent.

Case 2: Hitachi—Brazil

Prospecting Relationship Marketing (PRM)

Agency: Rapp Collins Brazil

Background
Hitachi Data Systems (HDS) is the leader in data storage solutions for the largest companies in the world. It has a 44 percent market share in final product storage. With the objective of serving the Brazilian market, HDS launched a new solution called SAN to safely store and expand corporate data.

Challenge
To generate demand for the SAN solution in a highly competitive market, increasing short-term sales, and building a qualified prospect base for the long term.

Solution
Starting with company and contact lists, a prequalification job was done through telemarketing with the objective of "cleaning" the available data. Then, a direct mailing with information about the SAN solution was sent to the base. Using the call-to-action technique, the interested parties were directed to a live site that was designed to assess their degree of interest (see Figures 9.7 to 9.10). The prospects were segmented as Hot A/B, Warm A/B, Cold A/B, and Cold C, using a registration form. The first group consisted of those who were interested in immediate contact with HDS and who had high potential for buying the solution. The second group differed from the first with regard to the desired contact time, which, in this case, was three months. The third group wanted to be contacted in six months. The fourth group was made up of those who had low purchasing potential and wanted to be contacted in the far distant future.

Figure 9.7 Direct-mail piece inviting prospects to register at the site and receive the gift.

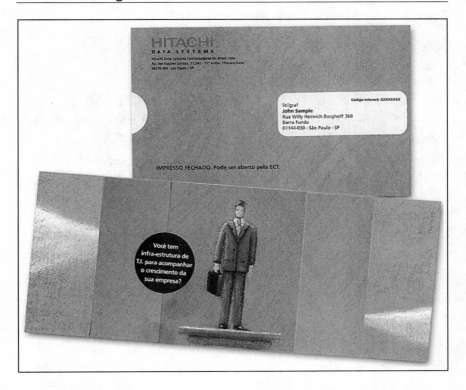

Figure 9.8 Interactivity of internal parts of the direct-mail piece.

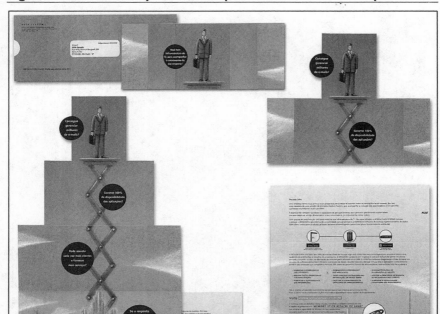

Figure 9.9 Registration site. Those who received the direct mail and are interested are registered at the site to receive the promotional gift and request a sales representative's visit.

Figure 9.10 E-mail piece inviting the user to visit the site.

Different contact strategies were developed for each of the segments. While the members of the first group received a scheduled visit by a sales representative, the relationship with the others was cultivated through online and offline communications, such as invitations to events and breakfasts with detailed presentations of the offer. In all cases, the contact history was filed in an online tool that managed the evolution of the base's interest in buying the SAN solution. No potential interested party was discarded from the base.

Results

The return from those who registered in the program was 19.6 percent. Of this total, 2 percent were classified as being in the Hot A/B segment, 4 percent in the Warm A/B, 7 percent in the Cold A/B, and the rest in the Cold C group. In a conventional demand generation program, all of these segments except the Hot A/B group would be discarded. Using PRM strategies as implemented in this case, no potential interested party is discarded. Management of the prospect's relationship cycle with the brand is guaranteed, and the relationship with the other groups is maintained, with the final objective of generating a visit by an HDS sale representative.

Case 3: McDonald's—Germany

Relationship Club

Agency: Rapp Collins Germany

Background

McDonald's Germany needed to develop a marketing strategy to obtain a long-term involvement with young consumers and at the same time reinforce the brand's image of being a "family-friendly restaurant."

Challenge

Gain children's loyalty in a competitive market and increase sales of the Junior Bag product for this segment. The results of the actions taken should increase short-term returns.

Solution

The McDonald's Junior Club for children and tweens from 4 to 12 years of age was created (see Figure 9.11). Two different versions were developed for all the communications, one for the 4- to 7-year-old segment, and the other for the 8- to 12-year-old segment. When a child joined the club, he or she received a welcome kit. The participants received a birthday card on their birthdays and a voucher for a free Junior Bag or a medium fries at any restaurant that participated in the program. They were also invited to celebrate their birthday at one of the McDonald's restaurants.

With the information on the participants in the club in the program's database, additional marketing activities could be developed, such as the opening of a new restaurant, summer parties, lightning promotions, and other such events. In particular, a direct communication was sent to support national Junior Bag promotions. When a club member reached the age of 13, he or she received a farewell communication and a voucher for a Big Mac.

Figure 9.11 McDonald's Junior Club.

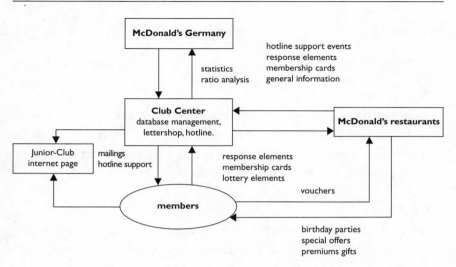

To promote dialogue with the children and their parents, the program used telemarketing and mailing address channels. Both of these instruments permitted the optimization of the club concept permanently. The club's Web site offered its members updated information on the program, online games, chat areas, and the possibility to exchange awards.

In a year and a half, participation reached approximately 810 restaurants and 700,000 associates. McDonald's Junior Club became one of the largest and most successful clubs for children in Europe. The response rate for promotions reached 25 percent on average, and birthday communications reached 80 percent. Sales rose more than 15 percent.

Case 4: NSPCC—UK

Nurturing a Long-Term Relationship

Agency: Rapp Collins UK

Background
The NSPCC's (National Society for the Prevention of Cruelty to Children) goal is to end child cruelty within a generation by developing a long-term integrated communications strategy that will grow donor relationships and maximize donations.

Challenge
More than half of the NSPCC's funds are gained through responsive, under-the-radar actions. With a constant focus on results, NSPCC wanted to introduce an updated relationship program that would nurture donors, with an eye toward

- Making them feel that their gifts had been appropriately recognized and valued, and used wisely
- Building the optimum relationship that met the needs of the donor
- Fostering the joy of giving
- Making them want to give again
- Optimizing lifetime value

Strategy
The NSPCC developed and launched a multimedia campaign encompassing DRTV, radio, direct mail, posters, radio, inserts, and door drops. The goal was to maximize growth of the donor file through recruitment, increase retention through regular giving, and build awareness of the issues (see Figure 9.12).

Results

- In 1996–1997 the donor program generated £9.3 million net income. By 2004–2005, this had increased by 303 percent to £37.5 million.
- Last year the donor relationship program raised more money than ever for children's services. Given the generally harsh environment for fund-raising, this marked increase in income has been astonishing.
- Additionally, the campaign has won creative excellence awards at the Institute for Fundraising, John Caples International, and Campaign Direct.

Figure 9.12 B2E: Posters that invite employees to watch the commercials that will run on TV in advance.

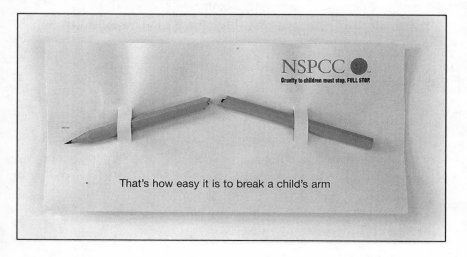

Case 5: Organon—Brazil

Integrated Communication

Agency: Rapp Collins Brazil

Background

Organon Laboratories, a strong specialist in women's care products that also works with various contraceptives, decided to launch a new vaginal sponge product, called NuvaRing, in Brazil. While NuvaRing had been very successful in several countries, it inaugurated a new segment in the local market for women's contraceptives.

Challenge

To position NuvaRing for doctors, resellers, and consumers as a new, modern, and innovative contraceptive method with the convenience of a single monthly application, something that women have always wanted.

Solution

Launch the campaign with integrated B2E, B2B, and B2C relationship communication. In order to add impact and credibility to the new method, the campaign used testimony from famous actresses chosen for having a representative typology for the target public. Specific actions were thus developed and directed to each key segment.

B2E (see Figures 9.13 and 9.14)

- Mobilize the Organon Laboratory team through internal communication and incentives.

Figure 9.13 B2E: Posters that invite employees to watch the commercials that will run on TV in advance.

Motivational poster
of the sales convention

Figure 9.14 B2E: Ground display at the sales convention.

B2B (see Figures 9.15 and 9.16)

- Involve medical leaders in gynecology.
- Hold a national convention and debate about the new product in a five-star hotel.
- Conduct a medical-clinical study with 4,400 doctors for their patients.
- Hold cultural events for doctors (with the presentation of the Black Swan Ballet).
- Engage in communications actions to the trade (distributors and drugstores) to prepare their sales channels.

B2C (see Figures 9.17 to 9.20)

- Launch the product for potential final consumers ranging from 17 to 35 years of age.
- Open a media campaign with DRTV, billboards, and magazines.
- Launch the NuvaClub educational Web site.
- Create educational teleconsulting.

Results

- Number of responses over the Web: 641,971
- Number of responses via telemarketing: 52,300
- Spontaneous recall: more than 80 percent
- Intention to talk with their doctor: 69 percent
- More than 105,000 users
- Sales growth rate: 50 percent per month

Figure 9.15 B2B: Disclosure material for drugstores and distributors.

Figure 9.16 B2B: Material for the Physicians.

Figure 9.17 B2C: Generate knowledge and interest. Magazine advertisement and display and leaflet for clinic.

Figure 9.18 B2C: Generate knowledge and interest. Film for TV and movies and banners for Internet.

Figure 9.19 B2C: Relationship. Site for registration; welcome e-mail and NuvaClub card given to user by doctor.

Figure 9.20 B2C: Relationship. Exclusive service for users, NuvaTime (member-get-member, users indicate friends).

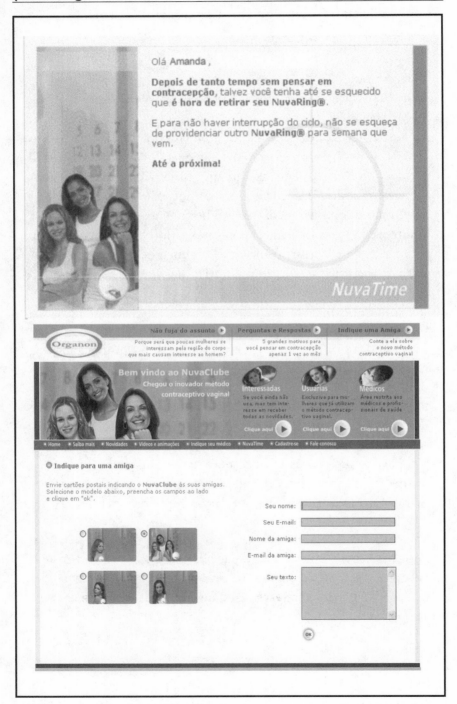

Case 6: Petrobras—Brazil

Communication Campaign through Social Networks

Agency: Rapp Collins Brazil

Background

Petrobras is the largest Brazilian company in the energy sector. In January 2007, it was classified by *Petroleum Intelligence Weekly* as the eighth largest petroleum company in the world. Just as Petrobras has been a technological pioneer in the exploration and production of petroleum and its derivatives and in the development of products, the company does not restrict its brand positioning to traditional media only. The company is investing more and more in new channels of communication in order to develop its relationship with stakeholders, among them investors, consumers, the third sector, communities, customers, suppliers, and the workforce.

Challenge

More and more people are sharing ideas and opinions about a range of topics on social networking sites, blogs, and virtual communities, using pictures or photos, links, text, music, and video files. For Petrobras, ignoring this space would be tantamount to discounting its importance as a channel to help the company consolidate the brand and do business with stakeholders. From this perspective, Petrobras tried to develop an outstanding presence in this environment, which reflects its concern with its constant search for innovative forms of relationships with its public.

Solution

Petrobras opted to start its presence in social networking through Second Life, a virtual community in which people, represented by personalized characters or avatars, may interact with one another and with different objects in the space. The company promoted a pioneering event in Brazil that involved the simultaneous participation of people from the real world and the virtual world. The event was a lecture, "Communication Technology: From Fiction to Reality," that explored the decisive role of virtual communities in marketing strategies and corporate communication. The event allowed the real-world audience and the people from Second Life to interact with each other and with the lecturer (see Figures 9.21 to 9.23). The presentation was recorded in podcast form and made available to interested parties. To participate in the event and receive the audio file with the content, individuals had to register their data. Those who could not participate because of space limitations also recorded their information for future contact.

Figure 9.21 Appearance of the virtual auditorium in Second Life.

Figure 9.22 Audience watching the presentation in Second Life.

Results

The ripple effect of the event was extraordinary. The main communication vehicles published the premiere of Petrobras in the virtual atmosphere, outlining the success of the solution. The company's stakeholders requested additional information about the new virtual relationship channel. The Internet community was abuzz about the event and its innovative style. As a result, Petrobras is developing a new strategy that calls for an even larger and more outstanding presence in this space.

Figure 9.23 Real-life speaker and his avatar.

Case 7: Pfizer—Brazil

Online Real-Time Monitoring Tool for Communication Channels

Agency: Rapp Collins Brazil

Background

Pfizer, which manufactures Viagra, implemented an educational relationship program for erectile dysfunction patients. The primary goals were to make the target public aware of the scientific advances in this area and to address any questions or concerns that it might have. Consequently, several communication channels were used, including direct mail, an online relationship portal, passive telemarketing systems, and advertisements with call to action in magazines, in newspapers, and on television. Vehicle coverage was national.

Challenge

To identify the best selection of channels for the different segments of the target public so as to optimize response rates and the return on the financial investment.

Solution

An online tool was developed to track public behavior in the different communications channels. All outbound actions directed the interested parties to central response systems based on an integrated telemarketing and Internet platform. The tool identified the effectiveness of each action in real time, analyzing the number of responses obtained and the necessary cost for development. The target public's demographic and psychographic attributes were compiled through online forms, questionnaires filled out by telephone solicitors, and geomarketing studies (see Figures 9.24 to 9.26).

Figure 9.24 Return in different channels. The online tool presents in real time the results from the communication campaigns in the different channels, including electronic and print media, direct mail, the Internet, and telemarketing. As a result, it is possible to calculate the ROI.

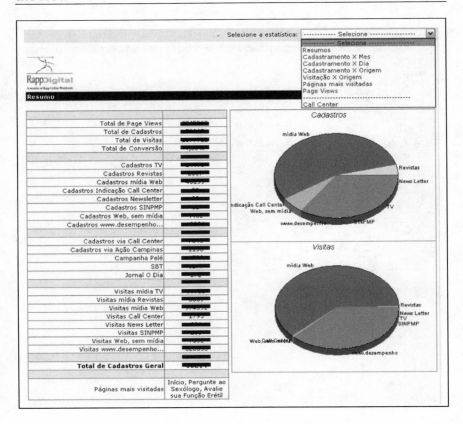

Figure 9.25 Reports. The tool allows daily follow-up of actions, enabling the analysis of the residual effect of each channel and the consequent need for new investments.

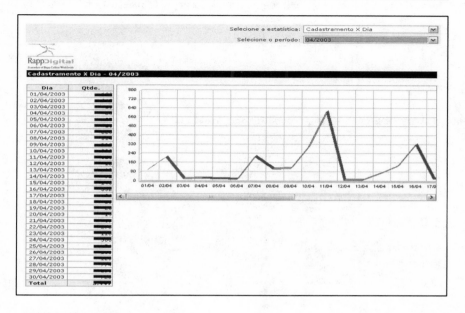

Figure 9.26 Behavioral map. Through the analysis based on geomarketing, it is possible to analyze how the different social classes in the target public responded to the communication actions.

Results

The follow-up allowed for a more thorough and accurate evaluation of the different segments' behavior, helping to identify the most appropriate channel for each group. Through real-time analysis of the responses, the effectiveness of the different vehicles could be tested, minimizing media costs and creating benchmarks for future actions.

Case 8: Philips—Brazil

Internet Sale Campaign

Agency: Rapp Collins Brazil

Background

Philips is a market leader in television sales in Brazil. The Internet plays an important role in its business strategy. By experimenting with its products in the virtual world, the company has attracted consumers to the brand and boosted online sales. In 2006, the company was a leader in consumer electronics sales in the online market.

Challenge

As it was about to launch a new line of standard flat-screen TVs, Philips faced fierce competition from companies that used low price strategies. Philips needed to emphasize the superiority of its solution in order to beat the competition and reach its sales goals.

Solution

The Internet was a fundamental part of that strategy. Through a promotional campaign, known as "Entre no Clima (Get into It)," Internet users were invited to enter a live site and learn the specs of the Philips flat-screen TV line in detail (see Figure 9.27). Those who bought the product won a number of DOTZ (online loyalty coupons that are often used by Brazilian Internet users) that they could exchange for several products, such as CDs, DVDs, and books. The size of the bonus depended on the value of the purchase.

To attract individuals to the promotion, the company used three public profiles. One consisted of Philips customers who had registered their information in the company's relationship

Figure 9.27 Hot site and banner for "Entre no Clima" campaign developed in Brazil to sell flat-screen TVs.

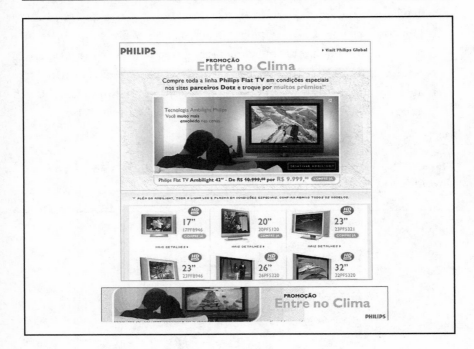

database and had already authorized new communications. A piece of marketing e-mail was sent to them, containing a link to the site that outlined the promotion and described the advantages of the offer.

The second profile included Internet users who were interested in the flat-screen TV line at a specific price. Those individuals, in general, are found through price comparison search engines and sites such as Buscapé. These individuals received promotions in online media via search engines.

The third group was composed of Philips employees. They received a marketing e-mail, sending those interested to a site with information about the product line and discounts.

Result

The company achieved significant sales, and the program became a marketing model that, with minor variations, was exported to other countries in Latin America (see Figures 9.28 to 9.30). In Argentina, for instance, the same strategy was used to leverage the sales of DVDRs. In Mexico, Philips repeated the action for Flat TV HD Ready products. In Chile, the company used the strategy to promote the sales of LCD and plasma televisions.

Figure 9.28 Hot site and banner for "Entre no Clima" campaign developed in Argentina to sell DVDRs.

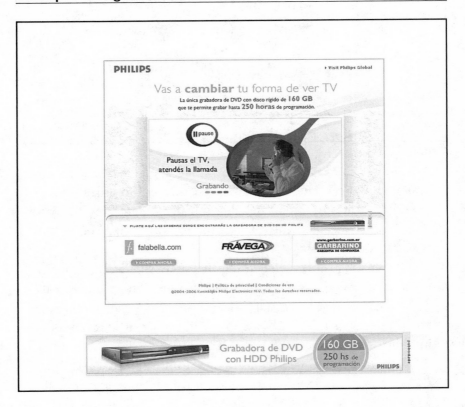

Figure 9.29 Hot site for "Entre no Clima" campaign developed in Mexico to sell flat-screen HD Ready TVs.

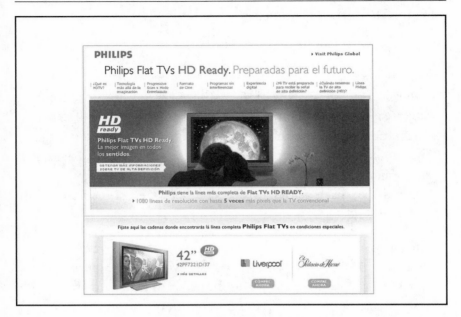

Figure 9.30 Hot site for "Natal Premiado" campaign developed in Chile to sell LCD and plasma TVs.

Case 9: Roche—Costa Rica

Loyalty/Retention Campaign

Agency: Rapp Collins Centro-America

Background
After Roche brought Xenical to the market using traditional advertising, surveys showed that there was a high level of experimentation, but few purchases. The surveys also pointed out that the product was not being used correctly, which worked against the brand and made the solution less competitive than cheaper methods. To make matters worse, doctors were not recommending the brand.

Challenge
To clearly position the product as a new weight-loss solution, not as just another weight-loss drug. In order to make a convincing case to the public, Xenical users were offered a full educational program with easy access channels. All of this was done with the involvement of doctors in the relevant specialty.

Solution
An integrated communication campaign geared toward both consumers and doctors in relevant specialties was developed, using a relationship strategy based on various actions, including direct mail, telemarketing, and the Internet. Xenical was positioned as a new weight-loss method, and the emphasis was on the benefits in physical appeal. Public loyalty was developed through an educational program and appropriate medical follow-up, easily accessed by the user (see Figures 9.31 to 9.33):

- Support for diet advice
- Psychological follow-up
- Continuous encouragement
- Professional medical advice

Figure 9.31 Relationship: welcomes sent after the joining the program. A series of educational guides with the objective of providing help and important information was sent to the patients who were already enrolled.

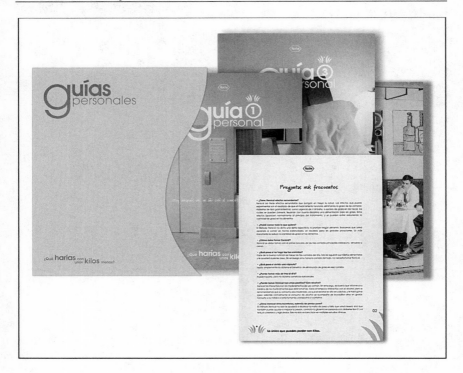

Figure 9.32 Home page of the Xenical Web site.

Figure 9.33 Guides: didactic content.

Roche

Comer fuera de casa

Comer fuera de casa es todo un reto al perder peso. Cuando se está con gente que disfruta deliciosos platos, es difícil no caer en la tentación. Hay dos aspectos importantes que tomar en cuenta: **cuánto comer y cómo responder al evento.**

Con un solo viaje a un restaurante, nadie se engorda. Aún una comida extraordinariamente grande de 5000 calorías, lo más que puede aumentarle su peso es 11/2 libras. Sin embargo, su respuesta emocional a esas calorías puede crear problemas. Las actitudes son tan importantes como las comidas.

A continuación le presentamos algunos consejos para limitar las comidas en los restaurantes. Usted también puede pensar en otras para agregar a la lista:

- **Pida una entrada o ensalada:** En vez de plato fuerte, busque primero en las entradas o ensaladas, si alguna de las opciones le gusta. Puede ser que sea lo suficientemente grande para que quede satisfecho.

- **Pida siempre a la carta:** A pesar del "buen negocio" de pedir el buffet, ya que usted termina comiendo cosas que no pensaba comer. Lo mismo para los "combos" o "comidas completas" de las comidas rápidas.

- **Divida las comidas:** Siempre es buena idea pedir un solo plato para dos personas, y normalmente alcanza. Otra buena técnica es pedir que le empaquen la mitad para llevar, antes de empezar a comer. Así no tiene la tentación de terminarlo.

- **Cuidado con el pan:** Siempre llega antes, cuando uno tiene hambre. Puede rehusar la canasta de pan, o bien hágala a un lado. Algunas personas utilizan el pan (sin mantequilla ni aceite), para aplacar el ataque de hambre y luego comer menos. Si cree que puede dominar esta técnica, inténtela, pero solo si va a evitar comer algo del plato.

- **Cuidado con los aderezos:** Normalmente son altos en grasa. Pídalo a un lado, o sin aderezo. También, no sienta pena si trae su propio aderezo sin grasa y lo utiliza.

- **Tome mucha agua:** El agua antes de la comida ocupará espacio en el estómago y le hará llenarse más rápidamente.

- **Los postres:** Lo puede comer si se cumplen dos condiciones: usted todavía tiene hambre, y guardó porciones del día para este momento. Considere opciones como fruta fresca o gelatina, tienen mucho menos calorías que los demás postres.

- **Cuidado con las calorías ocultas:** Las ricas salsas en los restaurantes franceses, los aceites en los italianos, los empanizados y los platillos fritos. Si no sabe qué contiene el plato, pregúntelo al mesero.

- **Cuidado con el alcohol:** Un whisky tiene 110 calorías y un coctel puede tener hasta 250. Prefiera vino blanco, o mejor aún, agua mineral o jugo de tomate.

- **La respuesta emocional:** Si comió más de lo planeado, no se desmorone. Repase las etapas anteriores y planee cómo se recuperará. Tampoco utilice este consejo como excusa para excederse todas las veces, mantenga la perspectiva.

04

Lo único que puedes perder son Kilos.

Results

A large contingent of customers responded and followed the program. In contrast to the nonparticipants, these customers increased their purchases and consumption periods at least fourfold. Sales volume also saw very positive results. There was less dependence on media advertising because customers were retained for a longer period of time. In addition, the participating customers tended to be strong multiplying agents through word-of-mouth advertising. Thanks to the results that they achieved with Xenical, they gave good recommendations to their personal and professional networks.

Case 10: Toyota U.S.

Increasing Customer Repurchase

Agency: Rapp Collins U.S.

Background
Toyota U.S. already communicates well with its current customers. In Q1 2006, the company had very good numbers in the industry, with a 61 percent repurchase loyalty rate, but in order to achieve its projection of sales volume of 3 million in 2010, it had to improve that rate even more. The company needed to be innovative in how it engaged owners and prospects, and it needed to talk to them in a tone, frequency, and pace that they would appreciate.

Challenge
To increase the number of repeat customers in the short term by identifying the number of Toyota owners and gradually increasing the number who return to Toyota rather than going elsewhere. Also, to drive car sales incrementally and deliver an acceptable ROI.

Solution
Toyota designed and executed a winning, integrated direct-marketing, call-to-action program that increased sales at a superior ROI by leveraging best practices in brand planning, analytics, contact management, creative execution, and direct-mail production (see Figures 9.34 to 9.37). The company also translated direct-marketing capabilities into actual, production-capable programs that performed in the marketplace.

The solution was broken down into several areas:

Figure 9.34 Buy direct mail.

Figure 9.35 Buy e-mail.

From: Toyota [Toyota@FromToyota.com]
Sent: Monday, September 18, 2006 4:22 PM
To: Walsh, Sheri
Subject: [CTEST1] Special 2006 Sienna Offers Inside

Cannot view this e-mail? See the latest offers now at toyota.com/specials.

GET UP TO $2,000 CASH BACK OR AS LOW AS 1.9% FINANCING* ON ANY NEW 2006 SIENNA FOR A LIMITED TIME.

BETTY, THE 2006 SIENNA. I SPY THE ULTIMATE FAMILY VEHICLE.

See all the great deals and financing specials at toyota.com/specials.

This deal is available at your local dealer(s):

• **DON JACOBS TOYOTA** – Map
5727 S. 27TH STREET, MILWAUKEE, WI
(414) 281-3100

• **WILDE TOYOTA** – Map
3225 SOUTH 108TH STREET, WEST ALLIS, WI
(414) 545-8010

There has never been a better time to get a 2006 SIENNA. Hurry in to your local Toyota dealer.

SIENNA HIGHLIGHTS

• Standard side curtain airbags on all three models†

• 60/40 Split & Stow 3rd Row™ seat provides flexibility

• Removable second-row modular seating with Front and Center™ middle-seat feature (8-passenger models only)††

• Dual power sliding side doors and rear hatch

• Available rear-seat DVD entertainment system with new 9-inch screen

• Available vehicle stability control (VSC)††

• 3.3-liter DOHC 215-hp V6 engine

CALCULATE YOUR PAYMENTS	SPECIAL TOYOTA OFFERS IN YOUR AREA	SEE THE ENTIRE TOYOTA LINEUP	VISIT THE SIENNA SITE

TOYOTA | *moving forward* ▸

Figure 9.36 Variable "buy" direct mail.

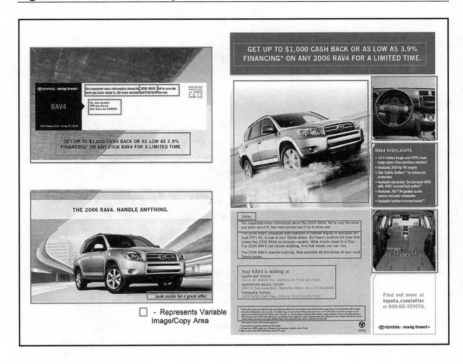

Figure 9.37 Variable "buy" e-mail.

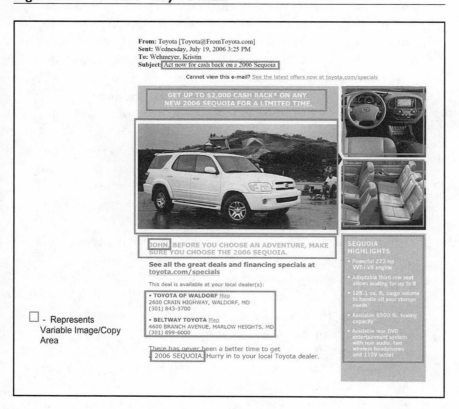

From: Toyota [Toyota@FromToyota.com]
Sent: Wednesday, July 19, 2006 3:25 PM
To: Wehmeyer, Kristin
Subject: Act now for cash back on a 2006 Sequoia

Cannot view this e-mail? See the latest offers now at toyota.com/specials

GET UP TO $2,000 CASH BACK* ON ANY NEW 2006 SEQUOIA FOR A LIMITED TIME.

JOHN, BEFORE YOU CHOOSE AN ADVENTURE, MAKE SURE YOU CHOOSE THE 2006 SEQUOIA.

See all the great deals and financing specials at toyota.com/specials

This deal is available at your local dealer(s):

• **TOYOTA OF WALDORF** Map
2600 CRAIN HIGHWAY, WALDORF, MD
(301) 843-3700

• **BELTWAY TOYOTA** Map
4600 BRANCH AVENUE, MARLOW HEIGHTS, MD
(301) 899-6000

There has never been a better time to get a 2006 SEQUOIA. Hurry in to your local Toyota dealer.

SEQUOIA HIGHLIGHTS

• Powerful 273-hp VVT-i V8 engine

• Adaptable third-row seat allows seating for up to 8

• 128.1 cu. ft. cargo volume to handle all your storage needs

• Available 6500 lb. towing capacity

• Available rear DVD entertainment system with rear audio, two wireless headphones and 115V outlet

☐ - Represents Variable Image/Copy Area

1. *Customer insight.* How to create a message that reaches someone who is in the market to buy a car. This has two components: how people move through the automotive experience cycle (from the time they buy a car to the time they get ready to buy the next one), and what inflection points matter, especially at the end of the cycle when the customer goes to buy a new car.
2. *Consolidating the data.* What data are available within the organization, and what can be collected to drive relevant communications.
3. *Targeting strategy.* What specific tools, particularly analytical ones, are needed to help identify specific owners, where they are, and what they need.
4. *Messaging strategy.* What content is relevant at what point in the cycle.
5. *Integrated creative.* How to deliver a message that is engaging and draws people in.
6. *Delivering customized communication.* Using technology and the available data, how to make the experience relevant and define the points where the customization of the communication is appropriate from a cost-benefit analysis.
7. *Annual contact plan.* How to align what messages are sent and to how many people in order to get the desired traffic to car dealers in a specific time frame.
8. *Results and learning.* How to optimize the program based on the learning process.

Results

- Targeting
  - In-market and loyalty models were validated and performed well in combination (40 percent improvement over 2004).
  - The program consistently delivered higher conversion rates (an average 8 to 15 percent incremental lift).

- Messaging
  - Sequenced shop and buy messages outperformed repetitive or ad hoc sales-focused messages.
- Offer
  - Preapproval offers delivered a consistent lift in vehicle sales and financial contracts (15 to 30 percent lift in financial contracts).

CHAPTER **10**

The Future of Marketing Communication

Increasingly, companies throughout the world are relying on relationship marketing to win and keep customers. This global trend is sustained by the history of its increasing representation in the communication mix and by the technological and socio-cultural factors that dictate the pace of its future advances.

History

The large marketing and communication conglomerates that have a global presence through their various agencies, (advertising, promotions, direct marketing, interactive and digital marketing, public relations, and branding) follow their clients' investments in the different communication areas to monitor changes in interest and expand the scope of their services. In 2004, *Advertising Age*[1] named the Omnicom Group, of which Rapp Collins is part, the top marketing and communications organization in the world, with annual earnings of more than $9.74 billion. This represents 30.8 percent of the total earnings of the other organizations in the top 25. In 2006, Omnicom's annual earnings reached $11.37 billion. The Omnicom Group has more than 1,500 agencies and companies operating in more than 100 countries. It has more than 5,000 clients, which include multinational companies and

single-country brands. (Those numbers attest to the comprehensive representation that this organization has in the marketing and communication setting.). Of its 2004 earnings, 34.5
percent were from customer relationship marketing (CRM).[2] In
2006, CRM represented about 36 percent of the total revenue.[3]
In other words, much of Omnicom's earnings stemmed from
relationship actions developed by its agencies for its clients. That
is more than one-third of the global investment in communication and marketing by brands!

In the future, technological advances and changing consumer
behavior and attitudes will make relationship marketing even
more pervasive in global communications. Thanks to the emergence of new relationship channels or networks, people will communicate more easily, which will enable messages to become
more direct and individualized.

Technology as an Agent in a New Culture

In only a decade from now, the computer as we know it will
disappear. It may become the size of a wallet or of the wall in a
house, according to Gates.[4] It could also come with special glasses
that will allow the user to see the outside world as well as watch
movies and read texts, says Jacob.[5] All personal and household
devices, such as watches, cell phones, PDAs, clothing, TVs,
DVDs, and lights, will have computers in them. And even more
impressive than the processing capacity will be the proliferation
of communication devices. Online and equipped with devices
called transponders, or chips that can be energized from a dis-
tance using radio waves, these devices will exchange information
easily to carry out tasks.

In a few isolated cases, we are already feeling the presence of
this technology in our lives today. Automatic tollbooths on

highways detect cars that have transponders installed on their windshields, receive each device's serial number information, and allow those vehicles to pass through. The entire process occurs without any human intervention until the final stage, when the amount charged is debited from the driver's current account. Futuristic ideas such as the refrigerator that identifies the end of the food stock and orders new supplies from the supermarket over the Internet and the car that receives an operation diagnosis for one of its malfunctioning parts from a self-correction network do not seem that far off.

In addition to the development of communication between objects, the interaction between objects and people will also undergo great change. Operating devices by using voice commands and recognizing people by using iris scanners are no longer the purview of science fiction. Safe processes for the identification of individuals through machines rather than using passwords and personal identification cards will be an everyday reality in the future.

People and machines will become part of communication networks, exchanging messages and information. Our bodies, our offices, and our homes will have networks. And they will all be interconnected, forming a giant web of relationships.

For companies, this generalized connection will permit individualized access to people to an unprecedented degree. The constant emergence of new devices linked to the network will imply the need to develop new communications languages to adapt the message to the environment. Direct communication with your target public will become increasingly intense. Individuals will interact with the brand, rather than passively watching product and service ads. The dialogue will result in the refinement of personalization procedures. Networks will record people's behavior to make the interaction between the brand and the base more relevant. Companies will store information about customers in their databases so that they can give those customers more personalized treatment. The importance of maintaining the privacy of individuals' data will become an ever more important issue. The knowledge acquired from the relationship should be used only to develop this interaction, and should not be passed on to other companies.

Technology advances at a very rapid pace. According to Moore's law, the number of components in circuit boards doubles every 18 months. Storage capacity on magnetic media grows 60 percent per year. Software is becoming increasingly sophisticated. The evolution of wireless networks will permit the integration of all machines in increasingly larger areas. The rate of technological evolution matches the projections made for the not-too-distant future.

The Strong Impact of Attitude and Behavior Changes

Although technology has played a key role in social and cultural advances, its impact becomes apparent only when people's attitudes toward the existing model change. History shows that there often is a lag between the occurrence of technological phenomena and the behavioral consequences that follow. In 1455, when Gutenberg revolutionized the way books and printed material were made, Europe was completely transformed by the invention. However, for the first 50 years, printed books contained the same religious content that monks had previously been writing by hand. According to Drucker,[6] about 7,000 books were published during that period, and most of them were traditional titles. The printing revolution that made information available on a wide scale and subsequently transformed society didn't occur until a half century later, when thousands of copies of Luther's Germanic Bible sold in a fraction of the time and at an extremely low price. During this same period, *The Prince*, by Machiavelli, the first western book published without a quotation from the Bible, was published. After that, books began to emerge on a wide variety of topics, such as literature, economics, and politics.

The Industrial Revolution followed the same pattern. Although mechanized production made a huge quantity of products available at low prices, for the first 50 years, the range of products created was practically the same as it had been in the preceding period. The great economic, social, and political effects were triggered only with the emergence of the railroads in 1829. First, they created a domestic economy in the United States, unifying once disconnected local and regional markets. Second, since they involved transportation companies with large-scale operations, they contributed to the creation of modern administration and accounting methods. People's geographic vision expanded, triggering the emergence of new products and markets.

Beginning in the mid-1940s, with the invention of the first modern computers, the information revolution set off the automation of a series of traditional processes. Companies, schools, and countless other organizations used software to manage their finances and operations and engineering projects, simulate natural events, and perform other functions. There is no doubt that technology has made it easier for humans to conduct all kinds of activities in a simpler and faster way. However, computers began to have the greatest impact on society in the mid-1990s, when the Internet became available for commercial use. Some historians even describe the Internet as the railroad of the new millennium.

A New Society

As virtual networks have improved and expanded, Internet user communities have eliminated geographic barriers. Millions of people from around the world are now connected through the Internet. According to Castells,[7] there were 400 million users in 2001 and 1 billion in 2005, and reliable projections indicate that there will be 2 billion people online by 2010. The availability of content and services has reached an unprecedented scale. Information about everything from medieval architecture to modern math, from environmental policy to macroeconomics, is available on Web sites. E-commerce has transcended the limitations of physical space, broadening the range of products and services offered on a global scale. People often do not know the geographic origin of the site from which they buy merchandise. But what is the importance of the point of sale's spatial location if the transaction process is all electronic?

The Internet has had a remarkable effect on consumers' attitudes and behavior. The exponential growth of content and services expands consumers' range of options. People can look for, analyze, and select the best choice from across the globe. They can have a dialogue with the brand through an interactive channel. Consumers no longer have to passively watch the offers being presented, but can interact at each stage of the relationship cycle. They decide the channel, the subject of interest, and how often they will interact with the brand.

These changes are having a major influence on how companies develop marketing strategies. The mass market is being replaced by the market of a single customer. Individuals expect to be treated in a unique manner and differentiated on the basis of their personal desires and objectives. Brands that promote interactivity change their marketing policies from those in which the focus is on the products to those that stress instead the relationship with the public. The product is good for serving the consumer market, not vice versa. The traditional value based on owning assets is transferred to conquering new means of access. The wealth of brands begins to be consolidated by building a customer base in which precise knowledge of those customers' demo-graphic, psychographic, and behavioral attributes sustains the building of on-target communication offers throughout the rela-tionship cycle, maximizing total LTV.

Transition-Period Barriers

When the Internet is used strictly as a mass communication vehicle, with messages designed to generate the highest possi-ble number of impressions, the vast opportunities of this new medium go untapped—and wasted. Using the Internet to sim-ply create virtual advertising is like publishing those first books during the print revolution or manufacturing those early products during the Industrial Revolution. It is using tradi-tional marketing techniques on a new medium with new possibilities.

When events and sales promotions are developed with the sole objective of generating immediate financial results, without gath-ering data from the participants to store in the company's data-base, a valuable opportunity for building long-term relationships is wasted.

When significant budgets are devoted to advertising in mass-market vehicles to build the brand, without trying to assess the campaign's impact on demand, the financial efficacy of mass advertising will remain a mystery.

When marketing campaigns use a mix of media—the Internet, advertising, direct mail, sales promotions, events, and public rela-tions—but each is kept as a separate activity, the target public receives a diluted message. To increase response rates, it is nec-essary to develop an integrated campaign in which each action boosts audience involvement, creating together a unified program and message.

The Future Is Based on Integrated Solutions with a Focus on Results

When integrated strategies are focused on the consumers—their needs and desires—the relationship-marketing program promotes an individualized dialogue with the target public. The company manages all points of contact with its base and is careful to allocate the most resources to those groups that offer higher value. By managing the various communication channels, the company ensures that its message is precise and synchronized.

At the same time that relationship marketing generates medium- and long-range results, it also reaps the benefits of short-term actions. In the first case, investments in developing relationship campaigns enhance the brand's image, which improves the customer's feelings about the brand. The more resources that are allocated to expanding and enriching databases, the more complete the picture of the target base becomes and the greater the possibility of sending successful messages. But it is not necessary to wait for medium- and long-range results to enjoy the returns on investments. Actions to generate short-term demand and sales can be implemented simultaneously to guarantee faster responses.

In relationship marketing, the results of all implemented programs are measured. Whether these programs are short, medium, or long range, the use of ROI models ensures that the analysis is sustained by financial indicators that compare the hypothetical projected returns with the real values achieved. Consequently, the actions can be continuously improved, using the highest benchmarks as reference points. The comparison among the returns from the different programs provides an objective platform for planning the allocation of future investments.

Relationship marketing is a solution to the problem of how to use new forms of communication and marketing in a new phase of social development. After approximately two decades of use, its global representativeness is supported by the high rates of return it provides to the companies using it. And the rates of return are projected to grow even more in the near future. As an innovative solution, it demands a vision that challenges traditional mass-marketing concepts to achieve tangible results. If this book contributes to the reader's participation in this new setting, it will have fulfilled its mission.

Key Points

- The growing use of relationship marketing to win prospects and keep consumers is a global trend. For example the Omnicom Group, of which Rapp Collins is a part, had annual earnings of more than $9.4 billion in 2004, and more than one-third of that came from relationship actions developed by Omnicom's 1,500 agencies for its more than 5,000 customers spread over more than 100 countries.
- Relationship marketing will become even more common in global communications in the coming years as a result of continued technological advances and changes in consumer attitudes and behaviors. The ease with which people will communicate thanks to the emergence of new relationship channels and networks will have a direct impact on the proliferation of direct and individualized messages. People and machines will become part of communication networks, exchanging messages and information. Our bodies, our offices, and our homes will be part of networks. And they will all be interconnected, forming a giant web of relationships.
- For companies, this generalized connection will permit individualized access to people in an unprecedented manner.

Direct communication with the target public will be increasingly intense. Individuals will interact with the brand rather than passively watching product and service ads. The consumer will define the frequency of the interaction, the channel, and the subject of interest. The impact of these changes on companies is at the core of marketing strategies.

- The mass market is replaced by the market of a single customer. Individuals expect to be treated in a unique manner and differentiated on the basis of their personal desires and objectives. The brands that promote this interaction will centralize their marketing activities and put the focus on the public, rather than using the traditional product-based perspective.

- Relationship marketing is a strategy for using a new form of communication and marketing in a new model of society. As an innovative solution, it demands a vision that challenges traditional mass-marketing concepts to achieve tangible results.

Insights on customers through segmentation: A case study in the wireless telecommunications sector

Behram Hansotia, president and CEO of Infoworks, a Rapp Collins company

As more companies began to develop an interest in using customer information to draw up their marketing strategies, the most frequently asked question changed from "Why should we use customer segmentation?" to "How should we use customer segmentation?" Before examining methodological issues, marketing professionals want to understand how segmentation can be useful in their work. This article will focus on a project in the wireless communications sector. In this case, segmentation was a process that had two main objectives: identify a group of customers' purchasing power and create retention strategies.

Information about the data

The data used in this segmentation included an expressive random sample of customer behavioral and demographic information obtained from an external reseller.

Developing segmentation based on the life stage

The objective of segmentation based on the life stage was to permit identifying purchasing strategies among prospects. However, only customer base data were used to relate the demographic and life stage characteristics to desired behaviors. The prospects were grouped into the same life stages. It was possible to compare the distribution of customer and prospect segments to identify the clusters of low penetration and high earnings (this defined their purchasing power).[1]

Some demographic dimensions, such as age, marital status, family income and existence of children, were initially defined through brainstorming sessions with the customer. All of the dimensions were then plotted in six segments according to the life stage, using the Latent Class Model. Customer penetration and distribution rates, as well as segment income, are represented in Figures 1 and 2, respectively.

Figure I   Penetration in Various Segments (by life stage) Compared to the General Population

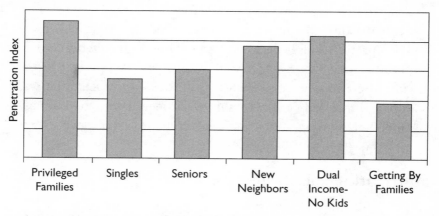

A high rate indicates a disproportionately large number of customers compared to the general population

Figure 2 Distribution of Customers and Incomes through Segments Identified by the Life Stage

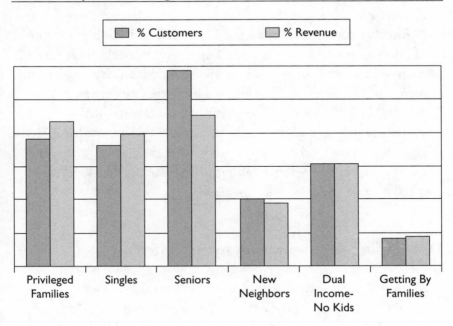

Recommended marketing actions for the segments

As shown in Figure 1, the segments with the lowest penetration were "Singles", "Senior Citizens" and "Prosperous Families". The company could choose "Prosperous Families" as a target segment, offering them several price plans, and the "Singles" segment, enticing them with a lower minimum monthly rate. Although the lower price plans would initially bring lower incomes with the "Singles" segment, these could grow right after acquisition. Furthermore, the opportunities for different creative versions geared towards these two segments became evident. The third segment with low penetration, the "Senior Citizens", was associated with low incomes per consumer, as shown in Figure 2. Therefore, there would be no high priority for acquisition efforts.

Another segment, "Privileged Families", had the highest rate of adolescent children at home. This segment could be reached using new models of portable devices and with price reduction plans during the off-season, when adolescents talk more.

The "New Neighbors" segment had a higher penetration of apartment dwellers who reside at the same address for at least two years and who tend to move. This segment could be reached using national or regional calling plans. Partnership marketing could also be used.

Developing segmentation by behavior

A multidimensional segmentation model was developed for customers using behavioral data as well as segments grouped according to their life stage (as one of the dimensions). The behavioral dimensions included the time during which the individual is a company customer, analogic versus digital telephones, the number of minutes used that exceed those included in the credit plan and the number of active services per account.

Customer dimensions serve as a basis for final segmentation. That's why they were carefully developed to provide considerable insight into the target public. Each dimension can be controlled as a mini-segmentation model, developed from a high level of customer contribution. Using the Latent Class Model, such dimensions were then plotted in five segments that described the customer base in a comprehensive manner. The description of these segments is in Table 1.

Table 1 Segment Description / Key Characteristic

Segment	Description/Key Characteristics
1. Communicative Families	• Families with accounts for several services • Above average incomes, payment of at least 8 dollars per month in additional resources • Above average use of roaming • Tend to make many short duration calls • Above average penetration in "Privileged Families"
2. New Customers	• Company customers for more than 3 years • Slightly below average income and tend to not exceed credit minutes • Most do not have demographic information
3. Convenience Users	• Customers of a single service with "Convenience" price plans • Use more than their permitted number of minutes • Higher proportion of weekend calls • High penetration in the "Singles" and "Prosperous Families" segments
4. Safety Comes First	• Customers have their phone for safety and guarantee reasons • The largest segment, but contributes little to total income • Customers for a long time • High penetration in the "Senior Citizens" segment
5. Super-users	• Tend to use several services, intensive use and higher income per account • High penetration of business customers (B2B) • Contains a smaller proportion of customers, but they contribute to a larger part of income • Most customers have digital price plans and exceed their credit limit • They bought their services through customer ownership channels or those controlled by them

Recommended marketing actions for the behavioral segments

Among all the segments, the "Safety Comes First" user category had the lowest incomes in proportion to its size (see Figure 3). These customers bought their phones for safety reasons and basically used them only in cases of emergency. Since this is the largest segment, but the one that also generates the least income, it was necessary to evaluate its profitability. The least profitable customers could migrate to pre-paid services.

Another segment, "Convenience Users", had many customers with fewer minutes than the average in their price plans, but they had a strong tendency to use more than those permitted minutes on a regular basis. Since the company's basic objective

Figure 3 Distribution of Customers and Income Using Behavioral Segments

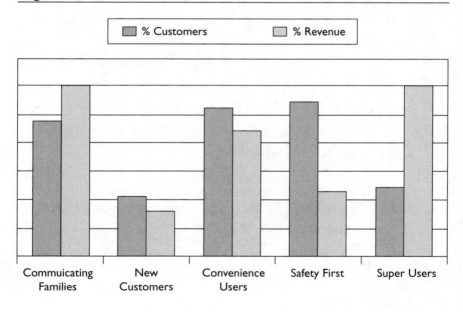

Figure 4 Three Dimensional Graph of Behavioral Segments. The size of the bubbles is proportional to the size of the segment

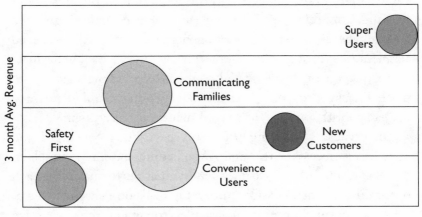

is to retain as many customers as possible, they could be recommended plans with a higher minimum monthly rate and more credit minutes.

The most valuable segments were "Communicative Families" and "Super-users", with the highest incomes in comparison to their size. "Communicative Families" had a lower percentage of customers with digital phones (see Figure 4).

Since the digital price plans are more convenient for the user (greater variety of price plans, better reception, etc.) and easier to be served by the company, it should be recommended to the analogic customers to migrate to digital services. The "Super-users" segment had higher utilization rates and higher expenses among all segments. These customers should receive special treatment and they should be rewarded through loyalty programs. The result: the company should do whatever is necessary to retain these customers.

Conclusion

Increasingly lower budgets and the reduction in response rates demand more relevant marketing campaigns, effectively directed towards the customer in order to generate profit. Well-conceived segmentation provides insight on the customer, which helps marketing professionals create and define offers and messages, elaborate loyalty programs, design new products and determine probable target publics for several marketing treatments.

Once these marketing programs have been conceived and tested, it is necessary to build response/income LTV models in order to foresee the customer's individual performance in each program. It is then possible to develop decision rules in order to select the optimal program for each customer and thus maximize financial performance. However, as a starting point, segmentation is the structure through which the companies can understand their consumer base and direct efforts with the objective of creating appropriate programs for different existing and potential customers.

Endnotes

Chapter 1

1. Terry G. Vavra, *Aftermarketing: How to Keep Customers for Life through Relationship Marketing* (New York: McGraw-Hill, 1995).
2. Web site: www.dell.com.br, April 2003.
3. According to a definition by the Direct Marketing Association (DMA), direct marketing is a marketing system that seeks a transaction or a measurable response from the consumer. Relationship marketing has a more comprehensive role: building a long-lasting relationship with the customer and, as a consequence, building brand loyalty and generating sales. Direct marketing thus finds itself within the scope of relationship-marketing programs, incorporating measuring capacity and the promise of obtaining results.
4. Stan Rapp and Tom Collins, *The Great Marketing Turnaround: The Age of the Individual—and How to Profit from It* (Englewood Cliffs, N.J.: Prentice Hall, 1990).
5. Don Peppers and Martha Rogers, *Enterprise One to One: Tools for Competing in the Interactive Age* (New York: Currency Doubleday, 1997).

Chapter 2

1. Booz Allen Hamilton Banking Survey, July 1996.
2. Jim Novo, *Drilling Down: Turning Customer Data into Profits with a Spreadshee.* (Deep South Publishing Company, 2000).
3. Frederick Newell, *Loyalty.com—Customer Relationship Management in the New Era of Internet Marketing* (New York: McGraw-Hill, 2000).

4. James L. Heskett, Thomas O. Jones, Gary W. Loveman, W. Earl Sasser, and Leonard A. Schlesinger, "Putting the Service-Profit Chain to Work," *Harvard Business Review*, 1994.
5. Ian Gordon, *Relationship Marketing—New Strategies, Techniques and Technologies to Win the Customers You Want and Keep Them Forever* (Toronto: John Wiley & Sons Canada, 1998).
6. David A. Aaker and Erich Joachimsthaler, *Brand Leadership* (New York: Free Press, 2000).
7. Torsten H. Nilson, *Competitive Branding* (New York: John Wiley & Sons, 1998).

Chapter 3

1. Malcolm Gladwell, *The Tipping Point—How Little Things Can Make a Big Difference* (Boston: Little, Brown, 2000).
2. Seth Godin, *Unleashing the Ideavirus* (Do You Zoom, Inc., 2000).
3. "Americas: AOL Must Put an End to Customer Default to Survive in Latin America," *Wall Street Journal*, October 7, 2002.
4. For online relationships as a counterpoint to offline relationships, refer to the use of the Internet as a virtual channel for dialogue between the brand and its target public.
5. Frederick Newell, *Loyalty.com—Customer Relationship Management in the New Era of Internet Marketing* (New York: McGraw-Hill, 2000).
6. Frederick Reichheld, and Thomas Teal, *The Loyalty Effect* (Boston: Harvard Business School Press, 1996).
7. Behram J. Hansotia, "Successful Customer Retention"; paper available on www.infoworks-chicago.com, 2001.

Chapter 4

1. Ernan Roman, *Integrated Direct Marketing* (Lincolnwood, Ill.: NTC Business Books, 2000).
2. João de Simoni, *Promoções de Vendas* (Pearson Education, 1997).
3. Edelman and Intelliseek, "Trust 'MEdia': How Real People Are Finally Being Heard," Spring 2005.
4. http://www.masternewmedia.org/news/2007/04/06/blog_usage_statistics_and_trends.htm, Abril 2007. Matéria: Blog usage statistics and trends: Technorati state of the blogosphere, fourth quarter 2006.
5. http://en.wikipedia.org/wiki/blogosphere.
6. Howard Rheingold, *The Virtual Community: Homesteading on the Electronic Frontier* (Reading, Mass.: Addison-Wesley, 1993).
7. http://en.wikipedia.org/wiki/list_of_social_networking_websites.

Chapter 5

1. Seth Godin, *Permission Marketing: Turning Strangers into Friends, and Friends into Customers* (New York: Simon & Schuster, 1999).
2. Bob Stone and Ron Jacobs, *Successful Direct Marketing Methods* (New York: McGraw-Hill, 2001).
3. Philip Evans and Thomas S. Wurster, *Blown to Bits* (Boston: Harvard Business School Press, 2000).
4. Stan Rapp and Tom Collins, *The Great Marketing Turnaround: The Age of the Individual—and How to Profit from It* (Prentice Hall, 1990).
5. David Shepard Associates, *The New Direct Marketing: How to Implement a Profit-Driven Database Marketing Strategy* (New York: McGraw-Hill, 1999).

Chapter 7

1. Seth Godin, *Permission Marketing: Turning Strangers into Friends, and Friends into Customers* (New York: Simon & Schuster, 1999).
2. Ernan Roman, *Integrated Direct Marketing* (Lincolnwood, Ill.: NTC Business Books, 2000).
3. As described in the article entitled "Overall View of Regression and Regression-like Models and their Application," by Behram Hansotia,

   Regression analysis is one of the most used techniques in Statistics and Marketing. Direct marketing professionals are more familiar with regression in the context of selecting customers and prospects for different marketing programs. A regression model, even if developed basically to select publics, and if carefully elaborated, can be used for at least three purposes. They are:
   a. Classify a file based on projected value, or score.
   b. With a few adjustments, it can be used to foresee the performance of the chosen names (typically, response rates).
   c. It can provide explanations about the characteristics of names with high scores. Thus, if it is a response model, it helps marketing professionals understand the characteristics of individuals with a greater probability of response, compared to those with a lower probability.

   The classic multiple regression model estimates the expected value of the interest variable, criterion or dependent variable as a linear function of a set of variables called predictors, or independent variables. The specific suppositions about the dependent variable and the nature of the function that relates the criterion variable to the predictors result in different types of regression. Source: www.infoworks-chicago.com.

4. Jim Novo, *Drilling Down: Turning Customer Data into Profits with a Spreadsheet* (Deep South Publishing Company, 2000).

Chapter 8

1. Behram J. Hansotia, "Enhancing Customer Value," white paper, Infoworks.
2. David Shepard Associates, *The New Direct Marketing: How to Implement a Profit-Driven Database Marketing Strategy* (New York: McGraw-Hill, 1999).

Chapter 10

1. FACTPACK 2006, Fourth Annual Guide to Advertising + Marketing, February 27, 2006.
2. The definition of CRM, or customer relationship marketing, is shown in literature as a set of concepts, constructions, and tools made up of strategy, process, hardware, and software [Miriam Bretzke, *Marketing de relacionamento em tempo real com CRM* (*Relationship marketing in real time with CRM*), (Editora Atlas, 2000). From this perspective, a great emphasis has been placed on exploring the technological, cultural, and systemic aspects for implementation. However, little attention has been given to communication itself, which feeds the interaction with the customer and keeps the relationship active. The reference to the CRM area, in this case, is related to all marketing activities needed to implement communication based on relationships with the target public. Only those forms that are based on mass communication strategies are disregarded.
3. For Omnicom's annual earnings, see http://files.liveadmaker.com/F/6327643/_OC266214551.pdf.
4. Bill Gates, "The invention of the digital wheel," *Veja*, September 2003.
5. Jean Paul Jacob, "Communications in the New Century: Invisible Computers," RNT, May 1999.
6. Peter F. Drucker, *Managing in the Next Society* (New York: Truman Talley Books, St. Martin's Press, 2002).
7. Manuel Castells, A Galáxia da Internet: Reflexões sobre a Internet, os Negócios, e a Sociedade (The Internet Galaxy: Reflections on the Internet, Business, and Society) (Oxford: Oxford University Press, 2001).

Appendix

1. Segment names and some data were changed to protect customer confidentiality.

Index